THE
DAYS
BEFORE
CHRISTMAS

HOW YOUR FAMILY CAN
PREPARE FOR THE
COMING OF JESUS

THE
DAYS
BEFORE
CHRISTMAS

W. A. POOVEY

Illustrations by Audrey Teeple

AUGSBURG PUBLISHING HOUSE
Minneapolis, Minnesota

THE DAYS BEFORE CHRISTMAS

Contents

About This Book

This book is divided into three parts. The first part is intended to give the reader some idea of the major emphases for the days before Christmas. The individual sections in this first part are especially suitable for reading to the family just before the Advent season or during the first week of this period.

The second part is intended to provide some family fun and entertainment, and at the same time, help each member to become more aware of the true meaning of Advent.

The third part of the book consists of a series of devotions based on four Advent-oriented Psalms. The devotions are primarily for family reading but will also serve as personal meditations.

The days before Christmas are busy days, filled with much activity. At the same time these are also God's days, a time for all Christians to become increasingly aware of what God has done for us in Christ. It is my hope that *The Days Before Christmas* may help bring you closer to him who is the real meaning of Christmas and all of life.

PART I

The Story of Advent

THE DAYS BEFORE CHRISTMAS

A cold wind is blowing from the north. The dark silhouette of leafless trees is etched against a grey sky. Flurries of snow flakes swirl along the ground like scouts looking for places where deeper snows can be piled. Winter is on its way. Is that your picture of the days before Christmas, of the period we call Advent?

Possibly so if you live at the right spot on the globe. But in some places of the world the Advent season means hot, dry weather. In some areas Christmas marks the beginning of summer. December may be cold, dry, wet, hot, pleasant, freezing, uncomfortable, depending on where you live. Our image of the days before Christmas has been dominated by stories like "A Christmas Carol" by Charles Dickens, and songs like "I'm Dreaming of a White Christmas." Advent really has nothing to do with the weather. It is a season for all the world.

So what is it all about? What images are we to carry in our minds if we are not to think of snow and sleigh rides and cold winds? Every small child knows the answer. The days before Christmas are days of *waiting*, of looking ahead, of anticipation. "Is Christmas tomorrow? Is it the next day? Well, when, mother, when?" the small voices demand. Sometimes, when you are young, it seems as if the days simply will not pass. It's almost as if the clock has stopped and the calendar has fallen asleep.

Older people are not quite in such a hurry. Indeed the weeks before Christmas may seem to move too fast, too swiftly. There is so much to be done, so many things to prepare before the great day arrives. And yet a little of the child remains in all of us. We too wait. We all look forward to the age-old announcement—Jesus Christ is born in Bethlehem of Judea.

And each year the message sounds as if the event is just about to happen. We all know it occurred almost 2000 years ago. We have the record all printed out for us in the gospels. And yet we think in terms of the present.

"Joy to the world, the Lord is come," we sing, not "has come." And in that classic carol, "O Little Town of Bethlehem" the last line of the first verse declares, "The hopes and fears of all the years are met in thee *tonight.*"

That is as it should be. Christianity is not merely belief that certain events once happened, but that they happened for us. The birth, death, and resurrection of Jesus occur in each heart, in each life. And so each year we wait for God's goodness to happen again, for God's Son to be born again.

Only now we have a clearer picture of what is to occur than did the people at the time of the first Christmas. The news of the birth of Jesus was unexpected. It was a surprise to almost everyone. Only Mary and Joseph and perhaps a few others had any idea of what was going to happen and even they were not completely sure. But we know the story. God is sending his Son for all people.

And so we can also *prepare.* The days of Advent are days of preparation. And that doesn't mean just Christmas shopping and the addressing of cards and the baking of Christmas goodies. It means preparing our hearts and lives for him, getting ready to hear the age-old story but also thinking that perhaps this year our Lord may be with us in person, that this may not only be the season of his first coming but of his second coming too.

So we wait and we get ready. We sing, "O come, O come Emmanuel, and ransom captive Israel." But we also sing:

> The Bridegroom comes, awake,
> Your lamps with gladness take;
> Alleluia!
> And for his marriage feast prepare,
> For ye must go to meet him there.

Waiting and preparing. That is the pattern for the days before Christmas, for Advent. It is a busy season, but a blessed season for every Christian.

THE ORIGIN OF ADVENT

Everyone knows that the New Year begins on January 1. Everyone, that is, except Christians. The Christian church year begins four Sundays before Christmas, which means either late in November or early in December. Such a state of affairs may seem very strange. Are we trying to get a head start on everybody else or are we just trying to be different?

A little thought will show that most organizations have their own calendars and that often they differ from the official one. The school year starts in September and ends in June, with vacation time filling in the rest of the year. Many businesses, for tax purposes, keep their records from July 1 to June 30. Even individuals have their own calendars, measuring their life span from their birth date or counting their married life from the day when both parties said, "I do."

So the church is not being different or difficult. It is simply being logical when it begins the church year before Christmas. If we followed the regular secular calendar, we would mark the death and resurrection of Jesus each year before we celebrated his birth. The church year is a convenient schedule to help Christians keep in mind all that God has done in Christ.

We know, of course, that there is no fixed schedule given in the Bible for a church calendar. The Bible does not mention Lent or Epiphany or Advent. Even such an important date as Easter is not fixed by the New Testament but is based on the Jewish observance of Passover. Since the Jewish calendar was based on the phases of the moon and our present secular calendar on revolutions of the sun, Easter is a movable feast.

We can understand why Christians did not set up an elaborate calendar at first. The church expected Jesus to return to this earth almost immediately after his ascension and his return would make all other celebrations superfluous. Moreover, the church was threatened with persecution from time to time and any elaborate celebration would just call attention to people who were trying to remain nameless.

But Christianity is not a religion of abstract ideas. It is "the story of the saving deeds of the Lord," as Ronald Jasper says in his book on the calendar and the lectionary. So it was natural that some people would want to keep special days to remind themselves of the great events in the life of Christ. We do this, too, with events such as birthdays and anniversaries in our own lives. We celebrate patriotic holidays and mark special causes such as Mother's Day and Arbor Day. It is only natural that believers in Christ would want to remember the important events in his life.

Easter was the first special day, followed by Epiphany on January 6 to mark the baptism of Jesus and the coming of the Wise Men. Later, especially by the churches in the West, December 25 was chosen as the birthday of Jesus, although we have no evidence that this is the actual date of his birth. December 25 was probably selected to replace and supersede a pagan festival. But step by step the Christian calendar began to evolve.

The days before Christmas had no special name and did not become a part of the calendar until comparatively late. But when Christians began to observe a special season of preparation for Easter, called Lent, it was only a matter of time before a season of preparation for Christmas became part of the calendar. The custom apparently originated in France or Spain and then spread to all parts of the church.

The exact amount of time to be observed varied for a long while. Among Eastern Christians, Advent often started on November 11, St. Martin's Day, and extended to Epiphany. But by the 8th century the practice we follow today was well established. Advent begins four Sundays before Christmas, which means that the new Christian year starts either on the last Sunday in November or the first Sunday in December.

The name "Advent," given to the days before Christmas, has a clear and simple meaning. Advent means "coming." Coming refers to the birth of Jesus who came to this earth on Christmas. Advent is our time of preparation before we celebrate the good news of the birth of Jesus. But the Christian church knows of a second coming of Jesus too, a coming in the future when he will return as he has promised. So the days before Christmas have a double emphasis—on a child who was born in a manger, and on a king who will return to rule and judge the world.

One of the problems with Christmas is that it won't

16

stay put. December 25 and the twelve days of Christmas that follow comprise the Christmas season. But Christmas keeps edging earlier into December and even into November. Christmas caroling and Christmas parties occur earlier each year, and we may grow tired of the whole business by the time Christmas actually arrives. Trees, manger scenes, music, and all the decorations we associate with December 25 illumine our store windows even before Thanksgiving.

Advent, a time of waiting and preparation, is confused with Christmas, a time of celebration. The days *before* Christmas tend to become the days *of* Christmas. This is unfortunate. Therefore we must work harder to keep alive the unique customs of Advent in our homes and in our churches. Let us use the days before Christmas wisely so that our lives and our hearts will be prepared to celebrate the birth of a Lord who will one day return to his people.

The Second Coming

A student is leaving for college. "Goodbye, goodbye," she says to all the members of the family. "I'll write often and I'll be coming home soon. Probably at Thanksgiving or maybe even before that."

A husband is leaving on a business trip that will take him far away from home. He fondly kisses his wife goodbye. "Don't worry, dear," he tells her. "I'll be all right. And I'll be home soon."

A general has suffered a military setback. He is being forced to evacuate the island stronghold where he and his men have fought so bravely. Squaring his shoulders he says to those who must remain behind, "I shall return."

Jesus Christ left this earth at the end of his mission and returned to his place with his heavenly Father. But before he left he informed his disciples, "Hereafter shall you see the Son of Man sitting on the right hand of power, and coming in the clouds of heaven" (Matthew 26:64). Jesus made the same promise that the student and the husband and the general made. He said in effect, "I'm going away but I shall come back." The second coming of Jesus is as simple as that. Only of course it isn't.

No one can doubt that Jesus made such a promise.

The gospel writers record it several times. The first preachers promised their converts that Jesus would return. And Christians in every age have looked for that return. At times people were so filled with expectation that they stopped working and sold all their property while they waited for Jesus. But Jesus has not returned. Now during the days before Christmas when we look forward to celebrating his first coming, how can we still talk about Jesus returning to this earth?

Well, it all depends. Why did the parents believe their daughter when she said she would be back? Why does the wife believe her husband? Why do the soldiers believe the general? In every case they believe the promise because they believe the person. And that is our answer to everyone who questions our faith in the second coming of Jesus. We believe the promise because we believe in the One who made it. No matter how long the return is delayed, we are sure it will happen because Jesus promised that he would return. And he has the power to fulfill that promise.

So the days before Christmas are also a special time to reflect on our Lord's second coming. Of course we must always be ready for his return, but in the time set aside to stress the events of Bethlehem, we also need to include the second coming as well as the first.

Sometimes the thought of Christ's return fills people with fright. They are like the housewife who is afraid that visitors will catch her with a dirty house. And Jesus did tell us, especially in his parables, to watch and to be prepared. But as emphasized in the New Testament, the second coming is presented as a promise, not a threat. This message has been a comfort to Christians in every age. In times of perse-cution the believers have looked eagerly for their Lord's return. Even when things are going well, the expectation that soon they will be even better has been a source of joy for Christians. While we look forward to the coming of Christmas each year, the possibility that this may be the great Christmas of our Lord's return makes our joy even much greater.

In addition, the promise of the second coming changes our whole perspective. Sometimes Christi-anity seems to be a religion completely rooted in the past. Important events have already happened. The Bible has been written and finished a long time ago. Salvation was won for human beings on the cross almost two thousand years ago. We are left with the hard work of policing the world after the big battles have been fought. We have the task of get-ting the news of what happened long ago to mil-lions of people now living in the world. Our work is important, but it doesn't seem as exciting as being present at Bethlehem or at the resurrection.

The second coming makes a difference. It reminds us that God's great actions aren't finished. We are not doomed to spend our time constantly raking through the ashes of the past. For there is still an-other date on God's calendar. We don't know the precise time he has written down for that event but we do know that there are still exciting things ahead. Jesus will return. The details need not bother us. We may be as confused and uncertain as those who looked for his first coming. But we believe our Lord's promises and we look forward with joy to the ful-fillment of those promises.

The people of the Old Testament went through a long Advent before Mary gave birth to Jesus. We rejoice that our Lord did come and win salvation for us. But in a sense we are in a similar position to those who lived before the first coming. We are waiting for an event of tremendous importance. God has promised it to us but he hasn't said when. So we watch and wait, and in the days before Christmas we pay special attention to the promises. Jesus has said, "I shall return," and we look forward with eagerness to that event.

> He who testifies to these things says, "Surely I am coming soon." Amen. Come, Lord Jesus!
> (Revelation 22:20)

Advent Now

Peter of Blois, a famous preacher of the 12th century, said in one of his sermons:

> There are three comings of our Lord: the first in the flesh, the second in the soul, the third at the judgment. . . . The first coming was humble and hidden, the second is mysterious and full of love, the third will be majestic and terrible. . . . In his first a Lamb; in his last a Lion; in the one in between the two, the tenderest of Friends.

Despite the neatness of this description, we are probably stuck with a numbering system which makes Jesus' return in glory the third coming. But the idea of a personal and individual coming between Bethlehem and the end is important for us, particularly during the days before Christmas.

For although Christianity is a religion with a strong emphasis on the past and the future, its most important stress is on the *now*. The question is always what is Jesus Christ to us *now?* Does he dwell within us *now?* This is the Advent that makes the first one important and the last one joyful. We need to love and trust him now.

There can be no doubt that Jesus seeks us and

wishes to come to us. He says that he stands at the door and knocks and will come in and sup with anyone who will open the door of the heart. Jesus invites those who labor and are heavy laden to come to him and he will give them rest. He promises to be living water in the heart of all who accept him. He is the Good Shepherd, the Door, the Vine. He often stresses his desire to live within the heart of each human being.

Yet his relationship to us is hard to define. Peter of Blois says this coming is mysterious, and he is right. It is difficult for anyone to say just why or how he became a Christian. It becomes even more difficult to understand the differences between human beings. Why does one choose Christ and another reject his invitation? Why did Judas alone among the twelve turn traitor? Why does the same person reject the gospel when it is offered and then accept Christ at a later date? No one can say. Phillips Brooks in his famous hymn, "O Little Town of Bethlehem" notes the mysterious nature of the gospel when he writes:

> How silently, how silently,
>   The wondrous Gift is given!
> So God imparts to human hearts
>   The blessings of his heaven.
> No ear may hear his coming,
>   But in this world of sin,
> Where meek souls will receive him, still
>   The dear Christ enters in.

But the second descriptive word Peter of Blois uses does help to explain this personal Advent. He says Christ's coming is "full of love." And the very nature of the gospel is contained in that phrase. Christ wants to come into our hearts because he loves human beings. There can be no other explanation for the whole story of Jesus. Only love would move someone to leave his high place in heaven and come to this earth as a human being. Only love can explain Jesus' willingness to suffer and die on a cross for people who had no appreciation for what he was doing for them.

C. S. Lewis in his famous book about devils, *The Screwtape Letters,* pictures the devils as wondering what God is up to in this world. It isn't possible, the devils think, for God to love such vermin as human beings. But it is not only possible but true. It is love that explains it all.

Indeed love is the key word for Advent and Christmas. And we all need to be reminded of that. For even in a season devoted to goodwill and peace among men we sometimes get disgusted with our fellow human beings. We would like to give some people a good shaking. We wish the preacher would really tell off the sinners. And perhaps he will. But harsh words won't change human beings. It is the hot sun of love, not the cold wind of denunciation that opens people's hearts.

Peter of Blois has one final picture about Advent *now* that is worth repeating. He describes the first coming as that of a lamb, and John the Baptist used that very word to describe Jesus—the lamb of God. He says that the return will be like that of a lion, and Jesus *is* called the lion of the tribe of Judah. But for the coming in between, Jesus is called the tenderest of Friends. Is there a more beautiful word to describe the relationship between our Lord and us than *friends?* Jesus used that word for the first time with his disciples on the night when he was betrayed, and it remains a word that all Christians can cherish. We even sing, "What a friend we have in Jesus." To be able to call our Savior and God also our friend is a rare privilege.

So the days before Christmas have a special meaning for each Christian. It is a time for looking within, for thinking about our personal relationship to Jesus. The days of Advent are usually busy days for everyone. But we need to take a little time to reflect on the one who is our guest all the time, the one who has promised to be with us to the close of the age. Once again Phillips Brooks can express our feelings in a striking manner.

> O holy Child of Bethlehem,
>   Descend to us, we pray;
> Cast out our sin, and enter in,
>   Be born in us today.

THE CUSTOMS OF ADVENT

Human beings like to celebrate and they like to develop special customs for special times. On St. Patrick's day many wear shamrocks or green neckties even though their ancestors never touched the Emerald Isle. On Thanksgiving day we decorate with pictures of turkeys and line our insides with pieces of that same bird. At New Year's Eve we represent the changing year with two symbols, an old man with a scythe and hour glass and a newborn baby to signalize the days ahead. So it goes.

Advent, however, hasn't managed to develop or retain many customs. The days before Christmas are so filled with secular and religious activities having to do with the celebration of Christ's birth that there is little time for special Advent customs. In Europe a few practices still linger but they are not well known in America.

The one custom best known here is the use of the Advent wreath. The wreath may date back to pagan times, to the original Germanic fire wheel, sacred to the sun god. As used today the wreath with its candles is a completely Christian custom and one that has found place in both church and home.

The wreath itself is usually made from greenery

with laurel, pine, holly, bayberry, or any other ever-
green. The wreath itself symbolizes eternity or the
all-encompassing love of God for the world.

In its simplest form the Advent wreath usually
has four candles, each one standing for a week in
the Advent season. In some instances a larger circle
is used with a separate candle for each of the days
before Christmas. In this case four larger candles
are used for the Sundays and smaller ones for each
week day. Such a wreath may not be practical in the
average sized home, however.

There is no complete agreement about the candles
themselves. Even the color is in dispute with one
writer insisting that three of them should be red,
although the more common color used is violet or
purple since this is the traditional color for Advent.
In many cases the fourth candle is white since this
one is lit on the Sunday closest to Christmas. Some
wreaths have a fifth candle in the center for lighting
on Christmas day.

In these days of electric lights it may seem a bit
strange to light candles in the home or the church,
but the flickering light of a candle has always had
a special fascination for people. Candles serve to
remind us of the true light of the world, Jesus Christ,
and so they have a special meaning in the days before Christmas.

Four candles mark the four weeks or Sundays in
Advent. Each week a new one is lighted as well as
those previously used, to symbolize the passage of
time and the approach to the day of Jesus' birth.

Probably there was originally no special significance to the individual lights, but over the years
each of the four has acquired a name. The first is
called The Prophecy Candle, reminding us of the

many statements in the Old Testament about the coming of Christ. The second candle bears the name The Bethlehem Candle, which refers to the prophecy in Micah 5:2 that the Messiah would come from Bethlehem. This is the passage that was read to the Wise Men when they came to Jerusalem seeking guidance.

Candle number three is called The Shepherds' Candle. The light of this candle symbolizes not only that the shepherds came to the manger, but that they went out and spread the news of Jesus' birth to others. The candle helps to remind us that we too are lights and that like the shepherds, we must tell others the true meaning of Christmas.

The fourth candle of Advent is The Angels' Candle. The world today doesn't talk much about angels, and that is understandable since we don't know much about them. But angels are signs of God's love and care. Angels told shepherds that Jesus was born. This fourth candle also reminds us of the abiding presence of God in our lives.

The simple symbolism behind the Advent wreath and the lighting of candles is an excellent reminder of the real purpose of the days before Christmas— a reminder of how God's Son came to this earth to bring us new light and life.

THE HYMNS OF
ADVENT

Someone once said he didn't care who wrote the nation's laws as long as he could write the songs. Songs have a way of lasting longer than laws and they are often more revealing of the real feelings of human beings. It would probably be possible to write a rather accurate history of the nation and of the church if one could make a study of songs that were most popular at any particular time.

Advent hymns are not numerous or very popular. Christian people have generally favored hymns that can be sung all year long, rather than those that are intended for a special season. Only the familiar Christmas carols have attained any great popularity among festival hymns. The four Sundays in Advent are too few to give Advent hymns enough exposure in the church.

Still, a few hymns intended for this season have become familiar to Christians. Among these we might list "O Come, O Come Emmanuel," "Come Thou Long Expected Jesus," "Wake, Awake, for Night Is Flying," "Lift Up Your Heads, Ye Mighty Gates," and "O How Shall I Receive Thee." When we look at these hymns, we see a pattern that tells us something about the proper mood and stress in the days before Christmas.

Advent has often been called an earlier or shorter Lent. But the hymns of Advent do not give that impression. Lenten hymns are often sad, slow, and written in a minor key. They reflect the sorrowful events that lead to Calvary. They also stress repentance and sorrow for sin.

Not so these Advent songs. They are all joyful, vibrant, lively. Descriptive words used in some hymnals to guide the organist and the congregation include "jubilant," "with spirit," and "vigorously." There should be time even in the days before Christmas for personal repentance and reflection, but as far as the hymns are concerned the mood for Advent is that of joy rather than sorrow or solemnity.

The Advent hymns are also strongly biblical in their language and imagery. "O Come, O Come, Emmanuel" stresses the idea of ransoming Israel. "Come, Thou Long Expected Jesus" also talks about Israel. "Wake, Awake for Night Is Flying" uses the parable of the wise and foolish virgins as the idea for the chorus. "Lift Up Your Heads" is based on the 24th Psalm, while "O How Shall I Receive Thee" employs the imagery of Palm Sunday. It is obvious that Advent is a biblical, not a secular season for the hymns are all rooted in the Old and the New Testaments.

But each song has its own story to tell, so let's look at them individually. The oldest one, at least as far as origin is concerned, is "O Come, O Come, Immanuel." This hymn goes back to a series of antiphons which were introduced into the vesper services about the 9th century. The antiphons were to be used from December 17 to December 23. Later these short sentences were worked into a hymn. Our English version first appeared in the 19th century and was the work of a remarkable hymnwriter and translator, John Mason Neale. Neale, a clergyman of the Church of England, studied carefully the hymns of the Latin and the Greek church and then produced some striking translations that sound like original compositions.

Neale's translation of "O Come, O Come, Emmanuel" emphasizes the Old Testament expectation of a Messiah. The names used for Jesus are all Old Testament concepts—Emmanuel, Rod of Jesse, Dayspring, Key of David. The last seems an odd expression, but it is meant to say that Jesus, son of David, has the key to heaven. The music to this hymn has a strange, soaring beauty about it.

Brother teams in the ministry are not uncommon. After all, the founders of Christianity include Peter and Andrew and James and John. But the two Wesley brothers rank high among family groups. John Wesley is the more famous, but Charles also left his mark on the church through his hymns. He is said to have written more than six thousand hymns. Some of these celebrate the coming of Jesus, and the one which has become a favorite is "Come, Thou Long Expected Jesus."

The hymn has only two stanzas, as printed in most hymnals. As might be expected, Charles Wesley stresses a personal message for Advent, although he too refers to Jesus as "Israel's strength and consolation." But he brings Jesus down to our age as he writes, "Born to reign in us forever," and later, "Rule in all our hearts alone." The warmth and personal emphasis of the Christian faith are reflected in this Advent hymn.

Few hymns have a more dramatic or tragic origin than "Wake, Awake for Night Is Flying." The writer, Philipp Nicolai, was a German Lutheran pastor in Westphalia at the close of the 16th century. In 1597 a terrible plague broke out in this German state, and Nicolai was forced to witness the death and burial of many of his parishioners. In one week 170 people died of the plague.

These tragic happenings did not drive Nicolai to despair, but moved him to write a book of meditations with the strange title *Mirror of Joy,* and included in this book was the Advent hymn. Nicolai not only wrote the words but also the music, a stately chorale which has been called the King of Chorales.

The words of the hymn reflect Nicolai's trust in God, even in the midst of terrible calamity. He uses the picture from Jesus' parable of the wise and foolish virgins, waiting for the bridegroom, a particularly good story for Advent. The hymn ends with a magnificent picture of heaven itself. It is too bad that such a hymn is sung, if at all, only a few times a year.

"Lift Up Your Heads, Ye Mighty Gates," is based on the 24th Psalm, one of the psalms often read in the days before Christmas. The words were written by a German Lutheran pastor, George Weissel who served a parish at Königsberg during the Thirty Years' War in Europe. Catherine Winkworth, the famous English translator, put this hymn into English and also did the translation of Philipp Nicolai's Advent hymn.

There is one special feature worth noting in Weissel's hymn. It not only emphasizes Christ's entry into the human heart but also says,

O blest the land, the city blest,
Where Christ the Ruler is confessed!

This is a thought that doesn't appear very often in Advent literature. Perhaps it would help if we could think of all government under Christ's control. That will not come completely until Christ's return but we need to keep in mind this wider vision.

One last hymn appears on our list, "O How Shall I Receive Thee?" It was written by Paul Gerhardt, one of the greatest of the German hymn writers. Gerhardt had a rather sad life, losing most of his family before he himself died. He was also put out of his church in Berlin because he refused to compromise with the government. Some of his own struggles are echoed in the final verse of the hymn.

Rejoice then, ye sad-hearted
Who sit in deepest gloom,
Who mourn o'er joys departed
And tremble at your doom,
He who alone can cheer you
Is standing at the door;
He brings his pity near you,
And bids you weep no more.

Yet the hymn is not a sad one, and the musical instructions say it should be sung "vigorously." For the Advent faith is a joyful one, despite personal sorrows.

The hymns written to be sung during the days before Christmas may never be listed among "My Ten Favorite Hymns," but they all underscore the message of a coming Savior and king. They are worth our study and meditation. Sing them at home during this season. Advent hymns make the message of the coming of Christ more personal and vital.

THE WHOLE PICTURE

Did you ever watch an artist paint a picture? The first few strokes may be very important, but they seldom give you much idea of what the final result will be. It is only when the picture is completed that you have a chance to see what was in the artist's mind.

The gospel story is very much like that. It begins with the message of Advent, with the strong voice of John the Baptist calling, "Repent! The King is coming." It moves to the simple and romantic story of the birth of Jesus in Bethlehem with its background of angels and shepherds and Wise Men. But if we stopped there, our conclusions would be misleading. For ahead in the gospels lies the ministry of Jesus, dominated by the dark shadow of Calvary, and ahead also lies the blinding light of the resurrection. It's only when we see the whole picture that we understand this Jesus whom we call Lord and Master.

So the days before Christmas are important, but they must be seen in perspective. They call for us to wait and prepare, but we are not just waiting and preparing for Christmas. Good Friday and Easter are on the horizon.

Strange that there must be suffering and death before God's work is accomplished. Why can't we have just Advent and Christmas? Why can't that dream of every child come true—Christmas every day or at least once a week? We cannot explain it, but it would seem that only out of suffering and death can true life appear. There must be anguish before there is joy. Even the first sound uttered by a human being is not a laugh but a cry. This is the law of the world.

Even the church's great hope of the second coming is hedged about with warnings of trouble and tribulation. Jesus predicted that there would be great suffering on the earth before his return, and certainly many people can testify that that sign has already been fulfilled. Wars and rumors of wars, pestilence, famine, and a thousand other woes have beset human beings in almost every age.

Still it is pleasant to think about the days before Christmas. They are busy but pleasant times in the home and in the church. There is a promise of peace and goodwill to all men in the air these days. In his famous *A Christmas Carol* Charles Dickens catches this mood when he pictures the ghost of Christmas present sprinkling a few drops of water from his torch on those who quarrel while making preparations for Christmas. Immediately the quarrelling stopped. *A Christmas Carol* is not a Christian story, but it captures the spirit of the season very well.

So perhaps we are not being foolish if we feel during Advent that the rest of the picture can wait for a little while. We need time each year to think about the good things God gives us, time to concentrate on the joy of Jesus' coming, whether we mean his first or second coming, or his coming to us in spirit now. The days before Christmas are not the whole picture. But they are an essential part of it. Let's enjoy, enjoy.

PART II

New Ways to Celebrate Advent

The days before Christmas are good days for family projects. As families we plan our gift making and gift giving. We plan our church and home Christmas celebrations. We organize to buy the tree and to decorate the house. Advent is a time for family togetherness, a time for family fun. This section offers ideas for family activity.

You may not be able to do all the things listed here in one season. This is a smorgasbord and each family will choose the activities that suit its particular needs. Every household should find something here to help prepare for the festival of good news at Christmas.

It is always difficult to gear such activities for small children, particularly those unable to read. But include all the family wherever possible. Small children can help make the Advent wreath and they can listen and learn as the others carry out the projects. If you write an Advent play, try to put in at least one line for each small child.

The important thing about the projects and games described here is that you try them. You may not always interest every member of the family but you will not know until you try. So liven up the days before Christmas. Pick out several things to do and try to get the whole family involved in a period of study and recreation.

Making and Using the Advent Wreath

The symbolism of the Advent wreath has been discussed in the first section of this book. Now let's see how the candles and wreath can be used in the home. The making of a wreath is a simple project and every member of the family can have a part. Some can gather the pine or spruce or whatever greenery is available. Others can construct a wire circle, perhaps out of a coat hanger, for the foundation of the wreath. The green material then should be woven or wired or tied to the ring. Be sure the branches are fresh, and relace them if they get too dry. Otherwise the wreath can be a fire hazard.

The four candles may be simply placed on candlesticks, inside or outside the wreath. Or they may be fastened to the wire in some fashion. Be sure to get long enough candles since at least one will burn every night for a four week period. It is possible of course simply to use four candles without the wreath. Lavender or purple candles are generally used with the fourth one perhaps white to emphasize the good news of Christmas.

Whether you use a wreath with candles, or just candles, make this Advent symbol the center of attention for family devotions. Each night ask a different member of the family to light the candle or candles for that week. Lighting can be done as you read the Bible verses for the meditation from the psalms to be used on this particular night. Or you may choose to read one of the prophecies from the Old Testament that speaks of the coming of Jesus. A list of such prophecies is appended to this chapter.

It is also possible to use each candle to express a special object of concern for the week. Perhaps the first week of Advent we will want to pray for and think about the members of the family, those at home and those far away. Each one present might offer a prayer during the week, or you might discuss what the coming of Jesus means to the family.

The second week might be devoted to thoughts and prayers about your church, asking God's blessing on church members and the various projects of the congregation. Thoughts about our nation and what the coming of Christ should mean to our leaders might be the theme for the third week of Advent. Prayers that God would guide our leaders as they seek for peace in the world would certainly be in place.

The final week before Christmas might be used to center attention on the people of the world, all those whom Jesus came to save. Remember our missionaries and fellow Christians in every land. You may choose other people and concerns for prayer in your family devotions. The important thing is to do something more than just light a candle. The glow of a candle is beautiful and it reminds us that Jesus is the light of the world, but we need to give each candle a special meaning during Advent.

Above all, don't make this time too solemn. Advent isn't intended to be a kind of early Lent. The coming of our Savior fills our hearts with joy. Make the days before Christmas happy days. Light a candle and let its light be reflected in your heart.

Passages of Prophecy to be used in lighting candles Deuteronomy 18:15, 18; Psalm 2:7, 8; Isaiah 7:14; 9:2; 9:6, 7; 11:1, 2; 25:8; 28:16; 35:1, 2; 40:5; 42:1-4; Jeremiah 31:33; Micah 5:2-4; Zechariah 9:9; Malachi 3:1; 4:5, 6; Matthew 1:21; Luke 1:17; 1:31-33; 1:68, 69; 1:76, 77.

Doing an Advent Play

The word "play" usually suggests a trip to the theater. Or it may remind us of a high school production or even a chancel drama in the church. But few people think of doing a play at home. Yet this can be a fine family activity for young and old alike. It is possible for the members of a household to write, costume, rehearse and produce a play, all for their own entertainment and instruction.

A play does not have to be a strange, exotic literary production. It may simply be a slice of life, a selection from our ordinary experiences and conversation. Shakespeare once wrote:

> All the world's a stage,
> And all the men and women merely players.

Even the lines in a play do not have to be memorized word for word. Today the schools are using a technique known as creative dramatics in which the characters know the plot of the play but simply make up the lines as they go along. You can do the same thing at home, so why not try producing a play as a before Christmas project for the family.

Of course each household will differ in the characters available. In some cases there will be a father, mother, and two boys. In another family the children may all be girls. This is another reason for each group to write a play to fit the people available. Of course it is possible for everyone to "double", that is, to play more than one part. You may indicate when a shift is made by a change in voice or by a costume change, putting on a different hat or a sweater.

We may wonder, if everyone is in the play, who will see it? But that's the wrong approach. The people in a play are the ones who have the fun and who learn the most from the experience. Of course if the family works out a good play, friends or relatives may be invited in to see the production. Perhaps a local church might be interested in seeing what the family has done. But the real fun comes in working out the production and in discussing the meanings involved.

How shall we start? Usually a playwright begins with an idea, the germ of a plot. From the plot he proceeds to the characters involved and then to the dialogue and action. After that the play is rehearsed and changes may be made to improve the presentation. Last of all comes the opening curtain and the actual production itself. You can have a world premiere right in your own home. One of the important things that a family can learn from producing a play is that each person has an important role in life. If four actors do their parts well but the fifth one messes up the part, the play is a failure.

Let's sketch out a play for a family to give you an example. We will use only two characters in this production. You can produce this play at home but you can probably work out a better one for your family.

First we need an idea. Suppose we start with a common task during the days before Christmas—

getting ready for the big day. Every household has things that must be done, cards to be mailed, decorations to be put up, and so forth. Suppose then we choose as our plot theme, "Getting Ready for Christmas."

We could develop the idea of someone who gets behind in the preparations and gets frustrated but is finally helped by the kindness of others. But this time let's take the opposite problem. Someone thinks she is all ready for Christmas but finds that many important things have been forgotten.

We will need some characters, two in this case. A mother-daughter arrangement is the simplest, although any two characters in a family will do. Let's decide that the daughter is the one who has completed all her holiday preparations, but she doesn't feel much like Christmas. The mother suggests some other tasks and these chores do the trick. There. We have a plot or story line, nothing big or dramatic, but enough to write a simple play. So here is our production.

Getting Ready for Christmas

(Setting: *A corner of the room.* MOTHER *is busy as* CLARA *enters.*)

CLARA: Mom, can I talk to you for a minute?

MOTHER: Of course, dear. You look worried. Something go wrong at school today?

CLARA: No, nothing like that. But you remember, last week I made out a list of things I wanted to do to get ready for Christmas?

MOTHER: Yes. That was a good idea. Are you having trouble doing the things?

CLARA: No. No trouble at all. They're all done.

MOTHER: Wonderful. You're all ready for Christmas then.

CLARA: No I'm not. At least—somehow I don't feel right about it.

MOTHER: What do you mean?

CLARA: Well, I've addressed all the Christmas cards and bought all the gifts for the family. I helped to put up the decorations and bake the Christmas cookies. But I don't feel like Christmas at all. I even played carols on my record player, and read Dickens' "Christmas Carol." But nothing seems to work.

MOTHER: Hm. That does seem a problem.

CLARA: Do you think I'm getting too old? Is Christmas only for young kids?

MOTHER: (Smiling) I'm sure it's not that, Clara. Let me look at your list. (CLARA hands her the list.) Tell me, did you write a letter to your Aunt Emma?

CLARA: I sent her a card like I did the rest of the people.

MOTHER: But she gets so lonely in that rest home and it's too far away for us to visit her very often. Don't you think you could write her a Christmas letter?

CLARA: Well, I suppose so.

MOTHER: (Looking at list) Is your school doing anything for a poor family this year?

CLARA: Oh yes, I forgot. We're supposed to bring some canned goods to school this Friday. I'll get some out of the cabinet right now. (Starts to go.)

MOTHER: (Stopping her) No you don't. You go down to the store and pick out some canned goods there. Something you buy special for them.

CLARA: Oh, all right.

MOTHER: By the way, did you learn your part for the Christmas program at church?

CLARA: I'm not going to be in the program. I told them I'm too old.

MOTHER: But they need help this year. Mrs. Wilson told me so. And so many at the church look forward to that Christmas program each year.

CLARA: I guess I'd better change my mind. Say, all of a sudden I'm not ready for Christmas after all. I've got a letter to write to Aunt Emma, some canned goods to buy, and a part in the program to learn. And you know what?

MOTHER: I think I can guess. But you tell me.

CLARA: I'm starting to feel a little of that Christmas spirit after all. And just when I've got lots to do. How come, Mom?

MOTHER: Well, the things you did before were just for us and for yourself. Now you're planning to do some things for others. Do you think that might make a difference?

CLARA: That's it. I guess Christmas isn't just a time for yourself. You've got to do something for others. And now I'd better get busy or Christmas will be here before I'm ready.

The End.

Such a simple play can be produced without a lot of memorizing. Just try to get the main ideas straight. Clear a space in the living room or dining room and present the play for the rest of the family. But this play suggests other plots you can work out. Here are three ideas.

1. What happened to Aunt Emma when she got a letter from Clara? Perhaps she had been fretting, thinking she had been forgotten. Or perhaps when

her letter arrived, someone in the home suggested that her niece wrote the letter because she was interested in her aunt's money. How did Emma answer that?

2. Clara and a classmate have the task of taking groceries to the poor family. What happened when they did this? Perhaps the poor people were proud and at first refused the gift. How did Clara handle this?

3. Clara does volunteer to help with the church Christmas program, but she doesn't get the part she wants. She is a bit hurt until she realizes that even our Lord gave up his place in heaven to come and help us.

Of course there are many other ideas for plays. Your family may like to do a biblical play with costumes and music. Dressing up is fun and the Bible offers us plenty of chances to expand on the stories. Here are two suggestions.

1. The shepherds in the Christmas story must have been talking about something before the angel appeared to them. Suppose they were discussing how long Israel had waited for a Messiah. Maybe they had given up on the idea. Then suddenly the angel appeared, and the long wait had come to an end.

2. What did Mary and Joseph talk about on the road to Bethlehem? All couples talk about the approaching birth of a baby. And this was such a special baby. Some of the conversation was probably very ordinary, some was filled with hidden meaning. End the play with the arrival in Bethlehem at the time Joseph is finally sure they will find lodging for the night.

The possibilities are endless. Doing a play is a good project for any family. It will heighten your appreciation of Christmas and the days of preparation for this great event. You will probably not rival Shakespeare with this production, but who cares. Try a play this year in the days before Christmas.

Living 2000 Years Ago

What was it like to live in a world where there were no electric lights, no television, no automobiles? What was life like in America in 1800? In 1700? Before the white man came to this land? It would be fun to travel in a time machine and go back to an earlier world. Since such a device hasn't been invented, we have to resort to other means to learn about the past.

Books and pictures are a help. Antiques give us some idea of how our ancestors lived. Reconstructed homes and villages such as Williamsburg, Va., allow many people to catch a glimpse of what life was like in colonial America. The past is probably a bit glamourized in such places but at least we can learn something about how people lived in the "good old days."

But what was life like in Jesus' day? Can we turn the clock back 2000 years and see what kind of a world our Savior was born into when he made his appearance in Bethlehem? Admittedly this is a harder job, for Jesus came into a land and a civilization far different from ours. Still, it might be fun to try to visualize that world. We can make a game of it and call it *turning back the clock* or *living 2000 years ago in Bethlehem.*

Of course we will have to let our imaginations roam a bit. Let's take a different room in the house each evening. Give each member of the family a pencil and paper. The younger members can have someone else write down a list for them. Players should list the things they think Jesus would also have had in his home and the things that he would have had to do without.

The radio and the TV will go on the second list immediately and so will electric lights and the daily newspaper. But don't sell the people short in that ancient world. They had books, although they were not like ours. They had rugs and dishes and the Romans even had running water, bathtubs, and toilets in some of their houses. But enough hints. Let each family member prepare the lists and then sit down and talk about them.

If you are undecided about some items, there are a lot of helps. Illustrations in the Bible or in Sunday school material may be useful although you must be careful in using pictures painted by famous artists because many artists pictured life as it was lived in their century, not in Jesus' day. Stories in the Bible may prove helpful. The parables of Jesus for example tell us that people in his day had coins and robes and rings. There are also books such as *The Way It Was in Bible Times* by Merrill T. Gilbertson that can give you authentic information if you need such help to make sure your lists are accurate.

But this is not just a game to see who can compile the most authentic picture of what life was like in Jesus' day. When we understand what kind of a world Jesus entered it should make us appreciate all the more his great love for us. Remember that he laid aside the glory and power that was his in heaven and came to that rather bleak world of 2000 years ago in order to save us from our sin. Moving from 20th century America to the stone age would be nothing compared to the sacrifice our Lord made.

There is another aspect of this game that should be discussed.

Advent is intended to turn our eyes toward the coming of Christ. But it will not hurt to take a few minutes to stop and think about the blessings we have because we live today rather than 2000 years ago. We called that world a "bleak world," and so it was. Most people lived short and hard lives. The government was cruel. Medical help was primitive or non-existent. Everything had to be done "in the sweat of man's brow." People who talk about "the good old days" certainly aren't talking about the world in which Jesus lived.

So when we finish the game and check our lists, it will not hurt to stop for a moment in prayer and say thanks for the blessings we have today. Christian people sometimes say we are too materialistic, too luxury-loving in our modern world. But that is true only when we forget the greater blessing—salvation in Christ. Let's thank God for what we have and end our prayer with thanks for God's greatest gift—Jesus Christ.

Future Unlimited

Jesus Christ is coming to this earth again. Anyone who reads and believes the words of the New Testament should be convinced of that fact. Jesus promised repeatedly that he would return. The apostles believed that their Lord would come back and they preached the message to all their hearers. The Christian church in every age has confessed: "He shall come again to judge the quick and the dead."

But what will life be like when Jesus returns? There is no clear description given in the Bible but there are hints and promises. The Bible speaks of a new heaven and new earth. We know that death and sin will be abolished. God promises to wipe away all tears from our eyes. Still, our ideas of that new age are a bit vague.

And perhaps that is as it should be. It will be nice to be surprised. Still, there are some good things in this earth that we hope will be retained in God's new kingdom. After all, God made the earth on which we live and he declared that it was very good. Even sin has not been able to destroy all the good things of life. No one would want to abolish a beautiful sunset or to destroy all the stirring music that human beings have written.

So maybe in the days before Christmas we should do some thinking about what we would like this new world to be like. This is a good topic for all of the members of the family to discuss together. What are the things in our present world that we would like abolished and what would we like to keep?

Why not have a talk session and try to make a list of the things we dislike and the things we still hope to find in the universe when Jesus returns? Have someone act as secretary to record the opinions of the family members.

Let's start on the list of bad things first. Probably everyone would put *war* at the top among things we can do without. Wars are cruel, stupid, and heart-breaking for those touched by a conflict. Already in the Old Testament people dreamed of a warless world as the great prophet Isaiah wrote:

> He shall judge between the nations, and shall decide for many peoples; and they shall beat their swords into plowshares, and their spears into pruning hooks; nation shall not lift up sword against nation, neither shall they learn war any more.

But war isn't the only unpleasant thing in our modern world. Pick up a newspaper and read the stories about trouble in every land. What other things should be eliminated? See how long a list you can make of the things that bother you in life. There may be some discussion about some of them. Parents may want to get rid of loud music; young people may disagree. But put down anything on which there is general agreement.

Reserve a special place on the list for the things we would like to get rid of in our own personal life.

Some may want the Lord to change their appearance. Others may list a bad temper, a weakness for alcohol, and others. When you get to this point perhaps each will want to make his or her own list, not wanting to admit weaknesses to others. But they probably know them already. Anyway, put down all the things you want abolished when Jesus makes all things new.

But God's new world isn't going to be a negative world in which certain bad things are absent. Sometimes our Christianity has that kind of negative slant and consists entirely of things we shouldn't do. But unless sinful actions are replaced by good actions, we will be like the man in the parable who got rid of a demon but ended up with seven other demons because his life was empty.

So let's make a second list. What good things do you hope Jesus will bring with him? What would you like to retain from the world in which we live? One example might be *friendship*. We would not want to live in a world or a universe of strangers. And the opportunities in God's new world will be so much greater than now because we can make friends with people who lived on this earth before or after us. Think of talking to Simon Peter or Martin Luther, or even the thief on the cross.

But there are certainly other blessings which we will expect or desire. This list should be as long or longer than the first one. But you need to let your imagination have full play. Dream a little. Perhaps it will help to read some sections from that strange book in the Bible, Revelation. Study the conclusion to the letters to each of the seven churches in the opening chapters. Read chapter 7 and 21 and 22. You may get some ideas from these descriptions of the new world. Discuss each item on the list with the other members of the family.

Of course this is not just a game to draw up a long list of items. Two good results can come from playing "Future Unlimited."

1. It should sharpen our desire to see the second coming of our Lord. Sometimes we get so entangled in the things of this life that we regard the return of Jesus as a threat, an interruption in life. But when we think of the real blessings that lie ahead, we look eagerly for the return.

2. When we look over our lists, we may be surprised at how many things can be changed right now. We can do something about hunger and poverty and sickness in the world. We can promote peace rather than war. Perhaps we need the example of the boy who heard his father pray that God would feed the hungry. The boy said, "If I had as much food as you have in the barn, I'd feed them myself."

Of course complete answer to life's problems comes only at the end. But while we look forward to the second coming, we can do the Lord's work now. Advent is the Christian New Year. Perhaps a few New Year's resolutions might come from playing "Future Unlimited."

Be a Poet

It is probably true that real poets are born, not made. At least some people seem to have a natural gift for writing in poetic language while others are like the man in Moliere's play who found that he had been speaking prose all his life.

Yet anyone can write a poem. Children in grade school have shown remarkable ability to express their thoughts in images and picture language. Adults, once they rid themselves of inhibitions, can write interesting verse. The result in each case is not great poetry but at least an expression of truth in a different style of language.

So why not have every member of the family write an Advent poem! Ask each one to do his or her own work and then at the dinner table or at family devotions read the results. It is wise to have each poem read aloud, for in poetry the sound of the language is more important than its appearance on a page. Perhaps a prize can be given for the best family poem or all the efforts can be exhibited on a bulletin board.

What kind of poetry shall we write? There are many varieties of course, but two general types will do for this Advent project. The more traditional type of poetry is rhymed verse that follows a rather rhythmic pattern. Thus a simple little ditty like this may be the type chosen.

> Advent! Advent!
> God's Son is sent
> To save you and me
> Eternally.

Rhyming poetry takes some skill, for often the words just won't fit. For example poets have been trying without success for many years to find a rhyme for "orange." Still, rhyming is fun and perhaps some members of the household will want to try it.

The second general type of poetry is free verse. Here the poet follows a fairly regular rhythmic pattern but makes no effort to find end rhymes. The psalms are good examples of this type of poetry. The poetic element is in the picture language used, not in the regularity of the verse. For example:

> John the Baptist.
> I don't think I would care to wear
> A camel's hair coat with a leather belt.
> And the thought of locusts mixed with honey
> Doesn't make me eager for dinner.
> Still, I would like to stand in the desert
> And call the sinners some scorching names—
> "Brood of vipers, hypocrites, liars,
> Take warning or prepare for fire."
> John the Baptist! He's my style.
> But before I start to shout and preach
> I'd better hear his call to me:
> "Repent, repent, the kingdom is near
> And the lamb of God has come for you."

What shall we write about? Advent is such a broad topic that there should be no difficulty in choosing a subject. Perhaps you can find a suggestion in the

following list, but don't be afraid to try something
entirely different.

> Advent candles
> Hanging the Advent wreath.
> Waiting for Christmas
> Waiting for Christ's return
> Waiting
> Sending Christmas cards
> John the Baptist.
> Christ with us everyday.
> A new heart for Advent
> December weather.
> Lonely people
> Sick relatives

The important thing is to give poetry a try. Even
if you live all alone, try your hand at it. A poem takes
only a pencil, a piece of paper, and an idea. Who
knows? You may write something that many people
will delight to read.

An Advent Quiz

Quizzes are fun. Everyone likes to pit his or her wits against others in the family or in a group. Of course when teachers give tests at school, that's not too pleasant because the students may fail the course. And trying to pass the written examination for a driver's license may prove to be a real chore. But simple quizzes at home can be very enjoyable.

If you have read all the material in the first part of this book, you can probably construct your own quiz about Advent. Your family may enjoy an informal question and answer time with each member in turn asking a question about the material which has been discussed in the meditation from the Psalms in Part III. You could compute scores and see who can stump the household.

Bible quizzes have special value because they not only test what we know about the scriptures but they also give us a chance to learn how to use the Bible when we look up the answers. So we are including a Bible quiz in this chapter, a question and answer examination about John the Baptist.

John was one of the great figures of the New Testament. Jesus paid him a high compliment by declaring that no man born of woman was greater than

John. Significant passages about John are found in all four gospels. The following are the major references to John the Baptist in the Bible. Matthew 3:1-15; 14:1-12; Mark 1:1-8; 6:16-29; Luke 1:5-24, 57-80; 3:1-20; John 1:19-36.

The following quiz can be taken by everyone at home. Make copies for all members of the family able to read. The trick is to try to get the correct answers without looking up the Bible passage. Score two points for every correct answer given. Then let the members of the family score one point for each answer that they get by looking up the material in the Bible. Perhaps a time limit might help speed the game and make the players hurry to get the correct answer. Note that in several instances the answer may vary, depending on which gospel reference you use.

A Quiz about John the Baptist

1. Who was John's father? Luke 1:59.
2. What did John's father do for a living? Luke 1:5.
3. Who was John's mother? Luke 1:13.
4. What prophet of the Old Testament spoke about John? Matt. 3:3; Luke 3:4.
5. What kind of food did John eat? Matthew 3:4.
6. Where was John baptizing? Matthew 3:1; Luke 3:3.
7. What did John call Jesus? John 1:36.
8. Name a disciple of John the Baptist who later followed Jesus. John 1:40.
9. Who arrested John the Baptist? Luke 3:19, 20.
10. What finally happened to John? Matthew 14:10, 11. Mark 6:28.

Try making up your own quizzes about Jesus or some of the Old Testament writers or about the Advent season. If you have a musical instrument in the house, have someone play the opening phrase of an Advent hymn and see who can identify it first. Remember, quizzes are fun. Shake the rust loose from your brain cells. Be a whiz with a quiz.

The Game of John the Baptist

One of the great figures in the Bible is John the Baptist or the Baptizer as he is sometimes called. John was the forerunner for the Messiah, the voice who announced the coming king, Jesus. Thus John is an Advent figure and his story is read in the church each year during the days before Christmas. Jesus said that John was the greatest man born up to that time and all four gospel writers tell, something about this forerunner.

John was known for his odd dress and diet, but even more for his sharp tongue. He spoke the truth in harsh and striking language even to the men who came from Jerusalem to inquire about his mission. Probably it was John's boldness that drew the crowds to hear him. John's sharp tongue finally resulted in his death but that is another story.

The Baptizer was a practical man and his religion was of the down-to-earth variety. He called on men and women to repent of their sins and he was not satisfied with people just saying that they were sorry. "Bear fruits that befit repentance," he said. In other words, don't just talk about repenting, show by your actions that you mean what you say.

When people asked him to be more specific, John spelled it all out so that no one could miss his meaning. "He that has two coats, let him share with him who has none, and he who has food, let him do likewise." John told tax collectors to collect no more than they were entitled to and he warned soldiers that they should rob no one by violence or false accusation but should be content with their pay. A very practical man, John the Baptist.

Now suppose we play a game, using John's down-to-earth methods of dealing with people. Let's bring John back to life again, in our 20th century world. He would certainly attract a crowd today, just as he did when he spoke to the people in Bible times. And his advice would be the same, "Repent of your sins and bear the fruits of repentance." But what would he tell us to do today? To answer that, we need to do some role playing, some acting out of different characters.

Here's how we play the game. Choose someone in the family to be John the Baptist. Then let someone else pick a certain profession or type of individual and face John in conversation. Let's try the game with one person being a student. The conversation might go something like this.

STUDENT: John, John the Bapist, can you help me?
JOHN: Only God can help you. But I am his servant. What do you want?
STUDENT: I am sorry for my sins. But you said everyone should do something to show that he is repentant. Well, what should I do? I'm a high school student. How do I show that I am repentant?
JOHN: That's not hard to do. Remember that other people are paying for your education, so study

hard and show you are grateful. Respect your teachers. Help your classmates, especially those who need friends or who may be handicapped in some way. That's my advice to you.

STUDENT: Thank you, John.

Let's take another example, which will help show how the game is to be played.

POLITICIAN: John, I want your help. I'm a representative in the state legislature.

JOHN: I can't help you get elected. That's not my business.

POLITICIAN: I'm not asking for votes. But I want you to tell me how I can show that I am repentant for my sins.

JOHN: Anyone can tell you that. You must always speak the truth.

POLITICIAN: Always?

JOHN: Always. People need leaders they can trust. Help all the people you serve, whether they're rich or poor. Don't take bribes. Be more concerned about the good of your country than the good of your party or your own good.

POLITICIAN: Thank you, John.

Now you get the idea. After each scene the whole family should talk about John's advice and see if it is the proper instruction for "the fruits of repentance." Take turns in playing the game and let everyone have a chance to be "John the Baptist."

Here are some suggestions of individuals who can be pictured as coming to John for help. You can add to the list. Remember that in every case the advice given should require evidence of repentance. Doing the things requested should always be understood as only that, nothing more. We do not save our souls by our own action. Salvation comes from the one whom John proclaimed, Jesus Christ. But here are some characters for the game.

A housewife.

A business man.

A laborer in a factory.

A college professor.

A stenographer in an office.

A waitress in a restaurant.

A soldier.

An airline hostess.

And many others.

The game of John the Baptist can be instructive for the whole family. It will help us to see our Christianity in very practical, concrete terms. Have fun and learn.

PART III

Advent
Devotions

It may seem strange to use selections from the book of Psalms as a basis for devotions in the Advent season. However, some of the psalms do reflect the Advent message of preparation for the coming of the Christ child just as effectively as other portions of Scripture. The church for a long time has chanted or read these Advent psalms as a part of the worship service.

Four psalms, the 8th, the 24th, the 42nd and the 111th are used as the basis for these devotions. The pattern of reading suggested is that on Sunday and the following Saturday the entire psalm is read, with shorter sections being used the rest of the week. The devotions are suitable for private reading or for family worship and each day's entry may be expanded by using Advent hymns and personal petitions in the prayers. If there is time, follow the reading of the devotions with family discussion.

Because of the peculiar nature of the Christian calendar, some years there are fewer days in the last week before Christmas. Seven devotions are nevertheless included here for that week. When Christmas comes early in the week, some devotions may be omitted or several may be read on the same night.

The Perfect Circle

"In the beginning, God. . . ." That's the way the
Bible starts. No arguments, no proof, no elaborate
deductions. Simply God. Genesis begins with the existence of God and it is interesting to note that no-
where in the Bible do you find any carefully worked
out proof for the existence of God. The Holy Writers
seemed to know that such a proof would be a waste
of time, that a God whose existence could be demon-
strated would be a God of our own making. God is
not the conclusion to a long argument. He simply is.

The author of the 8th psalm is in harmony with
this view. He too begins with God. He does speak
about the glories of nature and about the high place
of man in creation but in neither case does he use
this to demonstrate the existence of God. God is the
subject of the psalm, not the object to be examined
or tested. For the psalmist all things take their meaning from God, not the other way around.

It is only when we see this direction from God to
man that we can really understand the Bible. For
God is always the initiator, the mover, the beginner.
It is God who creates. It is God who condemns man
because of sin. It is God who plans a way for man's
salvation and who carries that plan into action. God
calls Abraham and Moses and all the prophets. And
finally it is the Holy Spirit who brings about the
birth of Jesus. Always, at every beginning there is
God.

And at the end, God. Note how neatly the author of Psalm 8 brings it all together by repeating the opening verse: "O Lord, our Lord, how majestic is thy name in all the earth." You might expect that the final sentence would say something about man since he is discussed toward the end of this beautiful hymn. But no, the writer returns to his first announcement. The whole history of the world lies between v. 1 and v. 9. But the message comes full circle or perfect circle. God is the Alpha and Omega, the beginning and the end.

So this is where Advent must begin. With God. Whether we think in terms of the approaching Christmas season or of the entire church year, we must begin with God. Before we try to carry out the popular slogan: "Put Christ back in Xmas," we must put God back into his world and into our lives. For God is the only right beginning for all the enterprises of man.

How clearly the brief poem by Maltbie D. Babcock puts it:

Back of the loaf is the snowy flour,
  And back of the flour the mill,
And back of the mill is the wheat and the shower,
  And the sun and the Father's will.

In the beginning, God. And in the end, God. Our entire existence is in his hands. Advent is a time of beginning and should remind us of the one who begins all things—God.

Heavenly Father, help me to say with the psalmist, "How majestic is thy name in all the earth!" May my life and all my actions find beginning and ending in you. Amen.

The Strange Ways of God

God seems to go out of his way to do things "the hard way." He picks a nation to be his chosen people and it turns out to be Israel, who he admits is the least among the nations. He selects a land for his people and chooses an area situated between the big nations of antiquity so that Israel is always being stomped on by Egypt or Assyria or Babylon. He decides to save the world and then allows his Son to be born in a stable and to be driven into exile almost immediately by a petty tyrant. Strange! Strange!

The psalmist notices this strangeness too. He notes that God finds strength and a bulwark, not in the strong ones of earth but in the chanting of little children. A fine defense! Is God foolish or is he just showing that he doesn't need man's help at all? Or is there another explanation?

Did you ever see a father lift up a small boy in a crowd and hold him above the heads of all the tall people? A father who does that is showing his love. The boy no longer feels trampled on, no longer inferior to those around him. "See how tall I am," he exclaims because his father has shared his own tallness with the boy.

That's a good picture of God in action. His use of the small and weak things of earth for his defense is an act of grace, a sign of love. God doesn't need help from babies or from giants. He can do it all by himself. But when he reaches down and uses us

75

in his work, we realize how concerned he is about us. Babes are his bulwark because he loves them, not because he needs them.

There is an old fable about a mouse and an elephant that walked across a rather flimsy bridge. When they got to the other side, the mouse said: "Boy, we sure did shake that bridge." And the elephant smiled and agreed.

This psalm, the 8th, is about the glory of God's universe and even about the glory of man. How comforting that at the very outset the writer mentions babes and infants so that we are not overwhelmed by the later verses.

Joseph F. Newton once wrote that if man had been planning the birth of Jesus, it would have gone like this:

> Army of Great Ones
> The Army marches by
> Fanfare of trumpets
> Enter the King!

But we weren't in charge of the script, and so Jesus came as a baby. Advent prepares us for the coming of God's strangest act—the birth of his Son. And perhaps it is only because God uses the weak things of life to confound the strong that we can feel safe with him. A terrible king would frighten us. A child, a man on a cross, can evoke our love and trust.

Lord God, you are so great and we are so small. But we offer you the little strength we have, confident that in your hands our little will become much and our weakness will be changed into power. Use us wherever we can be of service to you. Amen.

The Stars Speak

He stood on a lonely Judean hill and gazed at the heavens. He saw the moon rising majestically over the horizon. He saw the night sky almost covered with stars shining in the darkness. His feelings were those of Lorenzo in *The Merchant of Venice* who tells Jessica:

> How sweet the moonlight sleeps upon this bank!
> . . . Look how the floor of heaven
> Is thick inlaid with patens of bright gold.

The psalmist lived almost three thousand years ago and yet he saw the same sky you and I see every night. It says something about the permanence of this world and the mortal nature of man to realize that we still look at the same sky that he saw.

But did he see the same things we do? Certainly his understanding was not the same. The psalmist had no conception of the vast reaches of space. He did not know the chemical composition of the stars. He had never heard of a quasar or a nova; he had no idea what the dark side of the moon looks like. We have access to the secrets of the universe never glimpsed by people who lived B.C.

But listen! "Thy heavens, the work of thy fingers." "The moon and the stars which thou hast established." This early poet looked deeply into the universe. He was not dazzled by nature's magnificence. He saw the hand of God, he caught glimpses of the creator of all things.

What do we see when we look at the night sky? Are the heavens only the backdrop for our existence? Is the sky simply someplace where our airplanes can fly? Is space only an area to be explored by our rockets? If so, we aren't as wise as the psalmist even though he lived in a more primitive age. For mere technical knowledge is not nearly as important as the truth behind the universe.

Someone has said that the way to cure a man of being an atheist is to make him an astronomer for six months. That sounds very clever but it won't work unless a man learns to see more than the astronomer does. Behind all of this universe we must see the Maker.

And perhaps even that won't do by itself. Stars don't save anybody. Even belief in a master mechanic who made all things is futile until we also see God as the one who sent a Savior to this world. Advent is a time when we may be impressed by the beauties of nature but it is more important as a time when we think of God as one who prepared this world for the coming of his Son into our hearts and lives.

Lord, open my heart to the beauties of your creation. Let me see in every leaf and every star the evidences of your care. But help me to know above all the concern you have for me as shown in your Son Jesus Christ. Amen.

People, Not Things

How modern it all sounds. To the psalmist the universe seems so big and human beings seem so unimportant. "What is man that thou art mindful of him?" The words might have been spoken by an astronaut out in space, gazing back at the tiny ball we call the earth. The sentiment is one that might be expected from an astronomer or a scientist who has been studying the immensity of the universe. But the words were written by an ancient psalm writer.

The fact is that human beings have always felt this sense of alienation in the world. Somehow life seems too much for us. The universe is big, dazzling, and stable while we come and go. An earthquake can crush us, a tornado blow us away, a flood drown us. We seem like grasshoppers in God's sight, as Isaiah describes us. And if a writer in the Old Testament could have this feeling, how much more people today when there are so many more of us and we have such an understanding of the marvels of God's creation.

But such a view is all wrong. It springs from our being too much impressed by size and razzle dazzle. We are impressed by the Grand Canyon or the raging ocean and so we think God must be too. Surely he must be more concerned about the great things of the universe than about weak puny man.

That's nonsense. A God's-eye view of the creation

makes things look different. There is no big or small in God's sight. Jesus reminds us that God takes care of unimportant things like birds and lilies. In fact when one reads the Gospels it would almost seem that God works in reverse, showing more concern for little children and lame beggars than for the great things of the universe.

Moreover in God's sight the material things of creation are never as important as human beings, created in God's image. The Grand Canyon is a pile of rock carved by wind and water. The stars are fiercely-burning gas furnaces. What are they compared to a child with its potentiality for good or evil?

Some of God's attitude was reflected by an old woman who was unable to get out of her house. Fellow church members sent her presents at Christmas time and even cooked her a Christmas dinner. She thanked them for their kindness but then said, "It's people I want, not things."

God, too, is concerned about people. We may not be as pretty as a sunset or as strong as a tree. But God is concerned about man. We are his children, the masterpieces of his creation. We will always feel inferior when we look at the world around us. But when we look up, then we have no cause for fear. It's people God wants, not things.

Lord, in this Advent season, help me to feel your closeness, your concern. Keep me from doubting your love and help me live each day confident of your care. Amen.

How Great We Are

Psalm 8 has been called Genesis 1 set to music. That's a good description, for just as the opening chapter of the Bible reaches its climax in the creation of human beings, so this psalm finally sings the glory of man as God's finest creation. We are tempted to sing at this point, "How Great We Are."

What a picture! We are only a little less than God himself. We are crowned with glory and honor. We have been given the godlike power of rulership over all things on this earth. It's enough to make every human being burst with pride. How great we are.

And this is not just empty flattery. Human beings *are* a remarkable creation. Think of the wonderful accomplishments of the human race. People have written matchless poetry and beautiful music. Human beings have built great skyscrapers and tremendous power plants. We have penetrated the secrets of the atom and are busy discovering many of the mysteries of space. It is the fashion nowadays to speak critically of human accomplishments because of unfortunate effects on the environment, but we ought not forget the many wonderful things that human's have done. When we think of these things we are tempted to echo Hamlet's words, "What a piece of work is a man."

But there is a refrain in these three verses of the psalm. "Thou hast made him," "Thou hast given him," "Thou hast put. . . ." Man's greatness is a gift from God. Our superiority to all of nature is rooted in our dependence. We are in the same position as are all other parts of God's creation. We are a part of God's workmanship, just as the stars are and the minerals in the earth and the lowest vegetable or animal form of life. The glory all belongs to God.

It is this truth that men so often forget. One of the most interesting stories in the Old Testament is the one about King Nebuchadnezzar of Babylon who lost his kingdom when he said, "Is not this great Babylon which I have built by my mighty power?" Nebuchadnezzar did not return to his kingship until he learned to recognize that all things are a gift from God.

This story is a parable for all of us. Our greatness is not something we have by natural right, but it is the gift of God. And man loses the effect of his rulership when he begins to take credit himself for everything he does. Our song never dare be: "How Great We Are." In Advent and in every season of the church year we must learn to sing: "How Great Thou Art." For our glory is but the reflected glory of God.

Dear Lord, when we grow proud of our accomplishments and forgetful of your blessings, open our eyes to see the truth. Jolt us, if need be; shake us so that we are reminded that all good things come from you. Make us, above all, aware of your greatest gift to us—your Son Jesus Christ. Amen.

82

Read Psalm 8:4-5

The Ruins

Anyone who has travelled in Great Britain or Europe is aware of the existence of ruins. Here and there along the rivers or back from the highways or even in the center of the towns themselves, stand gaunt shells of buildings. Once life pulsed behind these walls. Once these ruins were magnificent mansions or churches or public buildings. Occasionally one can still catch a glimpse of the beauty which formerly existed. But generally today there are only gaping window arches, marred statuary and overgrown sections of masonry remaining.

When we look at human life, we are reminded of these old world ruins. For the picture given in Psalm 8 seems strangely at odds with what people really are like. We certainly don't seem a little lower than God. We are more inclined to think that human beings are like animals and we are aware that sometimes that statement is an insult to the animal world.

True, some semblance of the psalmist's view remains. Human beings possess minds that can make tremendous discoveries. Some people can write beautiful music or noble poetry. From time to time people manage to make a grand gesture and do a work of genuine charity. But these are only traces of the goodness that the writer of the 8th psalm talks about. Sin has been at work in our hearts. Man today is a ruin of what he was intended to be.

The realization of this may make us wish the

psalmist would be quiet, for his picture of man's greatness simply discourages us. It's like showing a bald-headed man a photo of him taken when he had a full head of hair. He would rather not be reminded of his former appearance. We too may be tempted to turn the page and say, "Why bother me with this picture of what man once was or was intended to be. That only makes the ruin harder to bear."

But of course this is where our comparison fails. For man is not like a stone ruin. A ruin cannot change, unless a restorer takes over and practically rebuilds the whole structure. But human beings can change. We do not need to remain ruins. What man was intended to be he can be through God's grace.

That's why this psalm is an Advent psalm. For Advent emphasizes change. It reminds us that something new was added when the Son of God came into this world. Jesus Christ came to restore the ruin that is man. "You shall call his name Jesus, for he will save his people from their sins" (Matt. 1:21). "I came that they may have life, and have it abundantly" (John 10:10).

So man as a person a little less than God, is not just a dream about a golden age in the past, or a glowing vision from never-never land. It is a clear statement of the intention of God, and Christ's coming was a fulfilling of that intention. The ruin *can* be restored. Our nature can be redeemed by the one we call Redeemer and friend.

Heavenly Father, we thank you for your gift of love in Christ Jesus. Without that gift, we are each a ruin, a helpless and sinful person. But you have made us new beings in Christ. Help us to live as restored and renewed people in your kingdom. Amen.

84

SATURDAY   *Read Psalm 8*

Look at Him

The Bible is divided into two sections, called testaments, and sometimes there doesn't seem to be any
real connection between them. The Old Testament
is all about the kings of Israel, the struggles of that
nation, and the literature that grew up in the time
known as B.C. The New Testament is all about Jesus
Christ and the church, and the chief connection
seems to be that Jesus lived in the same area that
the people of the Old Testament inhabited.

Of course that's all wrong. The two Testaments
form one book and the same God is worshiped by
people in A.D. and B.C. times. Someone once called
the Bible *The Book of the Acts of God* and that is a
good title. Moreover the Christian church has always seen Jesus Christ as the link between these
two sections of religious truth. Thus Jesus is the
second Adam, reversing the mistakes of the first.
Jesus is the new Moses, giving men the law of love.
He is the great king, outshining his ancestor, King
David. Jesus himself says of the writings of the Old
Testament: "It is they that bear witness to me."

So it is natural that men have seen a connection
between the 8th psalm and Jesus. Both 1 Corinthians
and Hebrews interpret the section dealing with all
things being subject to man as a description of our
Lord who will rule over all the universe. Jesus then
is the one made a little lower than God, when he

comes on this earth as a human being and he is the one to whom all things are subject.

Is that too subtle? Did the writers stretch a point to make the psalm fit Jesus? Not really. Such an interpretation reminds us that Jesus was totally and completely human. He represents what humanity was intended to be. Thus we are reminded that Jesus is our goal and our model as well as our Savior.

We need this picture of life. We are so surrounded by sin that we simply assume that it is an essential part of life. When we do something wrong we excuse ourselves by saying, "After all, I'm only human," as if humanity and sin are the same thing. Thus the message of psalm 8 makes us lift our sights. It makes us realize that it is Jesus who is human, not us. Our flaws and shortcomings are not examples of our humanity but of our failure to be what God intended us to be.

The beautiful words of this psalm then serve to remind us of a magnificent injunction in Hebrews: "Looking to Jesus the pioneer and perfecter of our faith" (Heb. 12:2). Advent means nothing without Christmas and Easter and Pentecost. So we turn our eyes toward Jesus and run toward him.

Jesus, you have shown us the way to live. You have given us power to serve. Help us in this Advent season to draw closer to you. Fill our hearts with good thoughts and our lives with good actions. Amen.

The Meeting Place

Where can we meet God? Where can he be found? In the Old Testament there was a simple answer to that question—in the temple at Jerusalem. God was there, not in the form of some idol, but he had promised his people that he would meet them there. Thus the 24th psalm describes two processions, worshipers going up to the temple to met God and the King of Glory entering to be with his people.

Of course the people of the Old Testament knew that God couldn't be confined to a building. The whole earth was his. Solomon said that heaven and the highest heaven couldn't contain God. Still there was comfort in knowing that there was one place where a worshiper could go and feel confident that God was there.

But where do we meet God? We are inclined to say quickly—the church. We even call the church building the house of God at times, and make it a substitute for the Old Testament temple. But Jesus put an end to such views. He indicated that God must now be worshiped in spirit and in truth. It is interesting to note that while God gave men of the Old Testament a definite plan as to how his house was to be built, there is no hint in the New Testament that we are even to build any kind of edifice for worship.

Where do we find God then? Certainly he is still to be found in his earth. Everywhere, if we look carefully we can see evidences of God's creative power. Whittaker Chambers, the former Communist, said that he first began to think about God when he noted the delicate convolutions of his little daughter's ear.

But more particularly we find God in other people. As we see what God can do in the lives of those around us, we feel his presence. Even when people are weak and sinful we can experience God in their presence because we come to realize his great love that even includes such human beings.

Someone has written a poem about a great mystic who wanted to find God. He separated himself from all human contacts and spent hours in prayer. He travelled to lonely places, hoping to experience the mystic presence of God. But all in vain. Finally he called out in despair: "Where are you, God?"

Then God replied from the midst of the busy city, "Here with my people, where I have always been." The poem makes its point very well. If we would meet God, we must be where he is, with people. This doesn't mean that there is no need for churches or worship services. It only means that we meet God and serve him when we meet and serve our fellow men.

Lord, be with me in this Advent season. Make your presence known. Help me to love others and to see you at work in their lives. Amen.

The Arrogance of Truth

The word *arrogance* may seem an unpleasant and unfortunate word to connect with *truth*. Yet there doesn't seem to be a better word to describe the attitude of people in both Old and New Testaments. Unfortunately in our translation "the Lord" conceals the cutting edge of this psalm. For Israel used the name "Yahweh" to describe God and what the psalmist was saying was that the only true God was Yahweh. The whole earth belonged to him.

And that certainly sounded like arrogance. For every nation in that day had a god. Each group sought special favors from its own deity but they were all willing to agree that Yahweh existed as the god of Israel. Only the people of Israel wouldn't have it that way. They insisted, "Our God is the only God. All the earth belongs to him. Our God is true, yours is false."

And that must have sounded arrogant to others, particularly when Israel was such a poor, weak nation. The Babylonians, the Assyrians, the Egyptians, the Persians, and later the Romans were the great powers in the ancient world. Yet the tiny nation Israel insisted that the whole earth belonged to their God.

That same conviction is found in Jesus in the New Testament. He insisted that he was the way, the truth, the life. He was the Door, the Good Shepherd; all others were thieves and robbers. If Jesus had been content merely to be another Jewish Rabbi with a few disciples, no one would have been disturbed. But he laid claim to being the very revelation of God himself and that was more than others could accept. "Who do you think you are?" they said, but Jesus stood his ground.

The church has not backed away from that claim today either. We still insist that we have the truth, the answer to human problems. We still talk to others about their faith and we send missionaries to lands to share our faith. We still preach that people come to God through Jesus Christ. There seems to be an arrogance about that.

And yet, of course, none of this is really arrogance. God's people in Old Testament times were not saying, "He's my God, not yours." And we dare not display an attitude of superiority when we witness to others. We must simply seek to share with others the grace God has given us.

A pagan woman, converted to Christianity said, "I have known him all my life. Now you have told me his name." That's what we seek to do—to tell others God's true name. In the Advent season, when we think of how the Lord has come to us, we want to remember others who also need the good news of the gospel. That's not arrogance but love.

Lord, keep me from being proud of my faith. Help me always to be thankful. Help me to show my thankfulness by sharing your truth with others. Amen.

Go Wash Your Hands!

"Go wash your hands before you come to the table." Every child has heard that injunction and millions of parents have given it. It is a call for cleanliness before blessing and that seems to be what the psalmist is saying as he lists the requirements for those who are to be admitted to the temple. Clean hands, pure heart, no false worship, no false swearing. Only people who live like that can come into God's house.

The words seem to echo those of Isaiah at the opening of his book when God denounces Israel's sins and then says:

> Wash yourselves; make yourselves clean; remove the evil of your doings from before my eyes; cease to do evil, learn to do good; seek justice, correct oppression (Isa. 1:16-17).

The point seems clear. Only good people should come to worship God.

But wait a minute. That doesn't sound right. It isn't in harmony with all we have learned elsewhere. God invites us to worship him in order that we can *become* clean. We come to God to receive forgiveness of our sins. But if we have to be clean before we go, there isn't any hope for us. How can these two views be reconciled?

The answer seems to be that you can't play fast and loose with God. You can't pretend to worship him and at the same time remain unrepentant and unchanged. What was bothering Isaiah was that Israel was carrying out all the ceremonies and at the same time was mocking God by continuing to do evil things. The psalmist too wants us to know that we can't get away with that.

One of the shocking things about the motion picture, "The Godfather" was that the gangsters in it continued to go through the rituals of the church, baptism, weddings, funerals, and at the same time went about their killing and robbing. That's a mockery of God. Yet even gangsters are not excluded from God's presence if they repent.

Advent is a season that emphasizes repentance. Advent is symbolized by John the Baptist who called for the people of his day to repent and prepare their hearts for the coming of the Messiah. We still call for repentance today, for purity and cleanness but the message is not "be worthy of God" but "let God make you clean."

Perhaps the perfect answer to the question of clean hands is the parable of the Pharisee and the Publican. The Pharisee was a better man morally than the publican but he was not good enough to stand in the temple since he did not see his sins. The publican was the one who belonged in God's house since he knew and felt his need for cleansing.

Lord, cleanse me. Take away the stain and guilt of this earth. Fill my mind with good thoughts, my mouth with good words, my life with good deeds. Amen.

He Won't Disappoint

There seems to be a nice pattern of promises and rewards in the Old Testament. Those who serve God get paid for it. As the psalmist says, the one with clean hands will receive blessings and vindication. The first psalm has the same stress—the good man "is like a tree planted by streams of water. . . . In all that he does, he prospers" (Psalm 1:3). It's almost like the seal act at the zoo; do the trick well and you get a tasty fish as a reward.

But life doesn't seem to fit that neat little pattern. Evil people aren't always punished, good ones aren't always vindicated. It was Christ who was crucified, not Pontius Pilate. It was Paul who was finally executed, not the people who brought false charges against him. Is the psalmist wrong or did things get out of hand after his day?

Neither of these alternatives contain the correct answer to our problem. There is a shift from material to spiritual promises between the two Testaments. But even in Old Testament times such books as Job and Ecclesiastes object that this automatic system of promises and rewards doesn't always seem to work. This does not mean however that the universe is in anarchy and that good and evil are of equal value.

What must not be overlooked is the simple word *when*. God's promises are sure and will be redeemed but the timetable is in his hand. We expect God

93

to function like the zoo keeper who automatically feeds the seal as soon as it has performed its trick. God is not like that. We can hold him to his word but we must let him decide *when*.

Perhaps the best illustration of this is found in the Advent message that Jesus is coming again to this earth. The early church expected his return almost immediately. They wanted instant blessing, instant vindication. Now we understand that only God knows when he will act. We have no cause to doubt the second coming. We simply must let God decide when.

The story of two farmers illustrates this very well. They lived side by side. One was a good man, the other an evil one. At harvest time the evil man sneered and said, "I didn't go to church. I swore and lied and cheated and yet I have just as good a crop as you do. Maybe even better."

The good farmer thought a moment and then replied: "God doesn't pay all his bills on the first day of October." Exactly. The Christian has no cause to doubt the ultimate justice of everything in this world. For God will not disappoint. The psalmist has not overstated his case. God will bless and vindicate those who serve him. But we must not be in a hurry, for the Lord is not. The *when* is his business.

Lord, teach me patience. Help me to trust completely in your love and your justice. When I am doubtful, remind me of your promise of a Savior and how you kept that promise. Teach me to trust in him. Amen.

Let's Play God

Would you like to play God? Would you like to run this universe for a little while? Most people dream of doing that from time to time. This world is always in such a terrible mess that we are tempted to believe that we could at least improve on things. Like the author of *The Rubaiyat*, we say,

> Ah Love! could you and I with Him conspire
> To grasp this sorry Scheme of Things entire,
>   Would not we shatter it to bits—and then
> Re-mould it nearer to the Heart's Desire!

There is one catch of course. If we were God, we would have to use naked power to accomplish our goals. People would have to be forced to stop doing certain things. Others might be forced to act, regardless of their desire to do so. Some people might even have to be eliminated entirely in order to make the world fit our plans.

And that's where we would differ from God himself. For God doesn't use force on human beings. He doesn't pull the strings and make us dance. He doesn't overwhelm man with his majesty and glory. He always gives us the right to reject and to refuse his desires.

Even in this 24th psalm with its magnificent ending, portraying the king of glory entering the temple, there is no force. God doesn't batter down the gates or storm the walls. The cry is "Lift up your heads, O gates! and be lifted up, O ancient doors." But there is no hint that those who control the entryway must act. The command to open can be defied and rejected if anyone wishes to do so.

This passage, seeking entrance by the King of kings, is strangely like the words of Jesus in Revelation in which he speaks of standing and knocking at the door of the human heart. For here too the decision to open or to refuse entrance lies with the one inside. Force is not used on anyone.

Sometimes people get exasperated at the church today when it follows God's ways. People want Christianity to use the techniques of the world in spreading the gospel. They think the church should use pressure, propaganda, lures, even force to get the customers in. For many, the method of preaching and witnessing seems hopelessly inefficient and old-fashioned. And of course it is, if we are seeking to force our way into other people's lives.

But God's method is that of friendly persuasion. It is the method of Advent which culminates in a baby in a manger. Part of the difficulty that human beings have in accepting Jesus is that he seems so low key, so soft-sell. But that's the way God works. He offers but doesn't compel. And it's alright for us to play God, if we only remember how *he* plays.

Dear Lord, give me the power to restrain power. Help me to trust in your wisdom and your ways, even when I find them hard to understand. Lead the church always to operate in harmony with your gracious way of reaching us. Amen.

Read Psalm 24:7-10

God on the Move

The famous writer, Thomas Carlyle once entertained a visitor who involved Carlyle in theological arguments about the nature of God. Finally the visitor said, "I can only believe in a God who does something."

Carlyle's face clouded up and he cried out, almost as in pain: "But he does nothing."

That's the way it seems sometimes, doesn't it? We pray and get no answer. We observe a world filled with violence and sin and God seems asleep. Evil grows stronger and God doesn't seem to raise a hand to help those who serve him.

But the picture of God as someone who does nothing is a false one. The writer of the 24th psalm certainly doesn't know anything about a God who stands still. Rather, he sees God on the move, advancing to the gates of the city and to the entrance of the temple. This God is alive and busy. He reflects Jesus' words: "My father works hitherto and I also work."

In fact if there's any one thing that the Bible seems to stress it is that God is a God of action. He played an active part in the entire history of Israel. He was involved in the whole work of redemption. And as the Holy Spirit God is pictured as still at work in the world and in the church.

Our difficulty isn't that God does nothing. It is simply that we can't see him at work. It just seems that he does nothing. But the people in Bible times weren't always aware that God was active; only after they looked back on events did they realize God had been involved. Think what happened at the Crucifixion. The disciples thought all their hopes were at an end. "We had hoped that he was the one to redeem Israel," the two men said on the road to Emmaus. But God *was* involved in the death and resurrection of his Son.

One of the unfortunate byproducts of scientific knowledge in our modern age is that as soon as we have discovered how some of the forces of nature work, we have divorced God from them. From such a false view it is only a short step to locking God out of his world completely and making him a God who does nothing.

That's all wrong. The message of Advent is the same as that of the 24th psalm—God is on the move. He is no celestial watch-maker who wound up his world and then forgot about it. He is a Father who is concerned about all his children and who is actively involved in all of life. We may only see through a glass darkly in this world but one truth we should never doubt. God is on the move in his world.

Lord, I do not ask to understand all your actions or even to be aware of them. But help me so that I will never doubt that you are with me every step of the way. Amen.

An Exciting God

A small boy sat enthralled as his Sunday school teacher told him the story of David and Goliath. When she finished by pointing out how God had been with David, the boy remarked, "God must have been more exciting in those days."

Sometimes it would seem that the boy was right. Certainly there is excitement in the 24th psalm. When we think of a procession of pilgrims going up to Jerusalem and chanting this psalm, it stirs us even today. And the great question and answer section at the end of the psalm with its final roar, "The Lord of hosts, he is the King of glory," has all the excitement of a football cheer.

A modern church service seems tame in comparison. The liturgy is often closer to what an old man called it, "the lethargy." The hymns often drag. The sermon seems a pale thing compared to the man who proclaimed the first Advent, John the Baptist. Have we run out of steam? Or is it God's fault for not being as exciting as he once was?

One thing we must not forget is that the Bible contains a selection of material gathered over a great many centuries. There were probably long periods in Bible times when things weren't too stirring. Moreover the exciting scenes aren't always the most important ones. Worshiping God is not an emotional jag. When God spoke to Elijah, his voice was not in the earthquake or the whirlwind but in the stillness which followed. Similarly our quiet daily devotional worship is often the best.

But having said all that, we still need to get excited about our faith from time to time. Advent is a time when some excitement is in order. Think of the message of this season. The One who came to this earth to save everyone now comes into our hearts. And he has promised to come again. The King of glory, the Lord of hosts is with us. That should stir our hearts.

An atheist once told a Christian that he didn't believe the confession of faith known as the Apostles' Creed and he didn't think Christians believed it either. When asked how he could make such a charge he replied, "If I believed that such things were true, I would shout them to the heavens. You mutter them as if they didn't matter."

Score one for the atheist. Our Christian truths are exciting. We have an exciting God, as this psalmist seemed to know. If we can get stirred by a football game, how much more should we feel a thrill of emotion when we think of the Lord of hosts who sent his Son to bring salvation and new life to all of us.

Lord, stir my heart this Advent season. Help me to grasp and to understand even a small part of your nature. Open my eyes to your glory. And fill my whole existence with your love. Amen.

100

Sail On

The American poet, Joaquin Miller is best remembered for his poem "Columbus." In the poem the first mate on Columbus' ship argues with the great admiral about the sea and begs him to turn back while there is time. But Columbus will not listen; in the face of every argument he gives the same answer: "Sail on! sail on! sail on and on!"

There is something of the same spirit in the 42nd psalm and in the one that follows it and may once have been a continuation of it. For this is a psalm of anguish, of discouragement, of apparent defeat. Enemies taunt the writer, memories burn in his mind, longings remain unfulfilled, and troubles seem to engulf him. But each section of the psalm ends with the refrain: "Hope in God; for I shall again praise him, my help and my God." The psalmist seems to be saying, in the midst of storms: "Sail on! sail on!"

This psalm forces us to face the fact that God has not promised us a rose garden. Temptations may come to us. Discouragements lurk. Even Jesus had to face the agony of Gethsemane and the torture of Calvary. But there can be only one answer to trouble —a stubborn determination to trust in God at all costs. In adversity we all need the determination of Job when he said, "The Lord gave and the Lord has taken away; blessed be the name of the Lord" (Job 1:21b).

Of course that's easier said than done. Anyone can

say, "Have courage," to someone else who is suffering. But consider the alternative. Would the psalmist have been better off if he had said, "I give up. I won't trust God anymore?" The negative response isn't much comfort. Being a cock-eyed optimist may seem foolish, but there's not much to be said for a dour pessimist. The psalmist had the right approach.

This may seem a strange psalm for Advent, but the mood has meaning for this season. Think of the people of Israel, waiting through the centuries for their Messiah. No doubt many of them felt as discouraged as the psalmist, yet there were always some who had this deep trust in God too. And they finally received an answer to their prayers.

We too wait for a coming Lord. And at times things look very discouraging. The world seems corrupt. The church seems lazy and meaningless. Our friends forget us. And the Lord delays his coming until we begin to wonder if he will ever return to his people. When we feel like that, we need to hear the refrain of the psalm, "Hope in God; for I shall again praise him, my help and my God."

Lord, at times I feel discouraged. Life seems hard and you seem far away. Give me strength to bear such thoughts. Remind me of your constant care and faithfulness and help me to walk by faith even when I do not see the way ahead. Amen.

God Hasn't Moved

"Where are you, God? Why don't you hear me? Why don't you answer me?" That's the way the psalmist felt. God seemed deaf to him, as deaf as Elijah said the false god Baal was to his priests. And it is a terrible thing when God doesn't seem to hear us. The psalmist was not alone in his experience. Isaiah said that God was a God who hides himself. Luther once grew so discouraged that his wife Katie donned mourning clothes and announced that God was dead. A famous Christian mystic once called this feeling of separation from God "the dark night of the soul."

At a time like the Advent season all of us may have a similar experience. We expect the nearness of Christmas to get our religious juices all stirred up. We are sure that carols and music will give us that "Christmas feeling." And often the old glow doesn't come. God seems as far from us as he did from the psalmist. Where is he? What's wrong?

Perhaps the answer is at least hinted at in a little story. A man and his wife were driving along in their car. The wife was in a reminiscent mood. "Remember, John, when we were younger, before we were married, how close we sat to one another when we drove? Now look at us. What's happened?"

The man glanced at his wife, from his position behind the wheel. "I don't know what's happened. I haven't moved." Perhaps that's an unfair answer between husband and wife but it is the proper answer as far as God is concerned. *God hasn't moved.* He's right where he always was. He's still to be found in his word and in his church, in prayer and in meditation.

The question always is—have we moved? Have we let things come between us and God? Remember in the parable of the sower how some seed fell among thorns and was choked out. The thorns represent the cares of the world, and the delight in riches and such things can certainly push us away from God. This is not to say that there may not be times when God withholds his blessing to test our faith and to show us whether we are serious in our prayers or not. But God doesn't move away from us. If there is movement, we are the ones who have shifted our position.

The season of Advent urges us to see if we have moved farther from God. Like building inspectors who check to see if there has been any movement in the structure of a building, Advent calls on us to check our foundations too. Are we standing where we belong—close to God? Are we aware of the Advent cry, "Repent, for the kingdom of God is at hand?" The checking is not difficult, but it is terribly important.

Lord, help me to stay close to you. Take away from my life anything which keeps me from your presence. Teach me to use the things of this world in such a way that they only make me realize all the more how you have blessed me. Amen.

The Enemy

One of the mysteries of life is why people should be opposed to the beliefs of others. If I choose to think that I once lived on the earth as a turtle, what is that to my neighbor? If I believe that my life is ruled by a six-handed giant who lives on a distant planet, why should my idea disturb others? Yet it does. There is something in faith that brings out the worst as well as the best in human beings.

The psalmist learned this the hard way. He was suffering exile and a sense of alienation from God. But part of his agony was caused by his enemies who reproached him with the question: "Where is your God?" Twice in this short psalm the writer records this taunt of his enemies.

The problem is a common one, faced by Christians in almost every age. Why should the leaders of Soviet Russia, for example, care whether their people worship God or not? Why should highly educated professors often feel moved to attack the church and the Christian beliefs of their students? It costs nothing to leave others alone. Our religion should be our own private business.

Yet, of course, that isn't true. Even if we make no move to convert others, and we must make such a move, the fact that we have faith and others don't is a reproach to them. They are afraid that the believer might be right and that is very disturbing. Few can follow the advice of Gamaliel who advised about the Christian movement, "For if this plan or this undertaking is of men, it will fail; but if it is of God, you will not be able to overthrow them. You might even be found opposing God!" (Acts 5:38-39).

Perhaps this tendency to oppose religious faith is the best witness of the existence of evil and of an evil power in the universe. How else can we explain that almost at his birth Jesus had to become a refugee? How else can we understand that when the perfect human being came on this earth they could find nothing better to do than to crucify him?

The Christian therefore must always be aware of this enemy who opposes him. There are people who don't like the message of Advent or Christmas. There are people who say worse things about Christianity than "Bah, Humbug," the words of Scrooge. The believer cannot relax with the feeling that all people are at least favorably inclined toward our faith.

A few years ago a newspaper carried the story of a man who had forcibly kept his wife from going to church. When asked for an explanation he declared: "I know I'm going to hell. I want to make sure she goes there with me." Unbelievable? Not when we are aware of the existence of the enemy.

Lord, keep me from evil attacks against my faith. Give strength to those who still endure persecution for their trust in you. And finally, give us all the victory over those who oppose you and us. Amen.

The God of Today

Memories! Memories are tiny sections of the past, imprisoned in our present life. Some are sweet, filled with the pleasantness of days that will not come again. Some memories are unpleasant and nightmarish, burning holes in our happiness. But strangely enough, the pleasant ones are often the most dangerous for they can catch us in a web of nostalgia that prevents us from facing the present.

The psalmist was in danger of falling into that trap. He had once been a joyful worshiper in the temple in Jerusalem. He had joined in religious processions, had even led the singing in the temple. And the memory of those days seemed to make his exile harder to bear. He was in danger of losing the present because it contrasted so with the past.

Memories are the records of things that once were but are no more. Memories are the ghosts of Christmas past, as old Scrooge found out. But God isn't a God of memories. His name is *I Am*, the eternal present, and his time is today. Human beings may think of religion as a nostalgic thing but God never does. He is the God of today and he is concerned about what we are now. It's today that counts.

There's good news and bad news in that fact. First, the good news. The emphasis on today means that there is forgiveness for the past. A woman who became a Christian put it well: "I feel like my sins were all on a big blackboard in heaven but God has erased

107

the blackboard." Exactly. The woman at the well had lived an immoral life, but she could be forgiven. Peter had denied his master but Jesus wiped out the past with the simple question: "Do you love me?" The great Old Testament prophet Isaiah put this truth in most striking language: "Though your sins are like scarlet, they shall be as white as snow; though they are red like crimson, they shall become like wool" (Isa. 1:18).

But this emphasis on the present can be bad news too. It means that we cannot run on memories. The fact that we once went to church, once believed and served God doesn't count. For God is concerned about our relationship to him now. He is the God of today. The psalmist's memories were of no value if they only helped him lose hope in God.

It isn't hard to see why God's emphasis should be on the present. What would you think of a person who said, "I once was an honest man"? Or of someone who confessed: "I once was a loyal American citizen."? Obviously we want people to be honest and loyal now. And God wants us to love him now. He doesn't live on memories. He's the God of today.

Lord, forgive all my sins and shortcomings. Stir my spirit so that I will love and serve you now. Turn my eyes and my thoughts away from the past and direct them toward you. Amen.

The Tides of Life

One of the most amusing religious books is C. S. Lewis' *Screwtape Letters,* the imaginary correspondence of a superior devil with his nephew Wormwood. In one chapter Screwtape explains that human beings are subject to recurring changes in mood and feeling. He calls this the law of *undulation,* the succession of troughs and peaks of spiritual response. Screwtape insists about man: "As long as he lives on earth, periods of emotional and bodily richness and liveliness will alternate with periods of numbness and poverty."

The writer of the 42nd psalm certainly seems to have been subject to the tides of life. Twice in this psalm and once in the section that follows he seems to have all his problems solved. He says, "Hope in God; for I shall again praise him, my help and my God." But the mood passes and he is plunged into despair again, only to move forward to a new statement of faith.

We can all sympathize with the psalmist, for we too know this sense of undulation, this ebb and flow of feeling. We have our spiritual ups and downs and they vary from person to person. For many, Christmas is the high spot of the Christian year with the carols and lights and the message of peace. But the joy ebbs away and often is replaced by loneliness and frustration. Ebb and flow, rise and fall, so it goes.

109

Two things are worth noting about these tides of faith. One is that we must learn to locate the cause of them within ourselves. The writer of the psalm enumerates all the external troubles that have upset him but he ends up talking to himself: "Why are you cast down, O my soul?" It's so easy to blame others when we are depressed. It's God's fault, or the church, or the members of our family. But faith rises and falls within us.

The second truth is that the law of undulation warns us to be constantly on our guard. The warning in the Bible is that the one who thinks he is standing is at that moment in danger of falling. Moses broke the Ten Commandments just after he had been in God's very presence. Jesus was tempted in the wilderness immediately following the exaltation of his baptism and God's testimony from heaven. Peter denied Christ the same night he bragged that he would never desert his Lord.

The wise mariner reads the tides. He knows what they can do and he prepares for them. There are tides for us too. Advent and Lent are seasons for repentance and a deeping of faith. We need to make use of them, knowing that the troughs may quickly follow the peaks.

Lord, I always love you. Sometimes I grow weary and my faith becomes weak. Help me through those experiences and let me grow stronger each day. Amen.

The Thing Called Hope

Christian and Hopeful were in Doubting-Castle, prisoners of Giant Despair. They were almost at the point of death when Christian said, "What a fool I am thus to lie in a stinking dungeon when I may as well walk at liberty. I have a key in my bosom called Promise that will, I am persuaded, open any lock in Doubting-Castle."

The scene is from *Pilgrim's Progress,* John Bunyan's great allegory, and it pictures Christian as coming to the same solution to trouble that the author of the 42nd psalm discovered. The answer is in the word *Hope.* "Hope in God," says the psalmist. There is no more beautiful word in the English language than the word *hope.* Hope is the key to overcoming trouble and continuing to move ahead. Sometimes hope is the key to life itself. When a situation is deemed hopeless, there is not much use in continuing to exist.

George Forell in an article entitled "The Christian Life Style" reports the observations of a psychiatrist who was confined in a concentration camp. The psychiatrist reported that those who thought and talked about the past were less likely to survive than those who were planning what they would do when they were released from the camp. Hope furnished a reason for continued existence, even under terrible conditions.

Yet this hope dare not be the senseless optimism of

111

Mr. Micawber who always expected something to turn up. A false sense of hope can be the sure way into the hands of Giant Despair. Some people seem to dwell forever in a fool's paradise. Hope has to have a reason, a goal, someone to give it meaning. The psalmist hopes in God and only there can people find help.

As is often true, living in the New Testament has tremendous advantages over the world of B.C. The psalmist hoped in God but his reasons for that hope were not as great as ours are. He had only glimpses of God's love. We have the witness of the cross. He knew very little about life after death. We have the story of the resurrection of our Lord to guide us. We live in the full light of the gospel of love. There is no cause for us to despair.

Paul, writing to the Romans, indicated the whole purpose of the Old Testament: "For whatever was written in former days was written for our instruction, that by steadfastness and by the encouragement of the scriptures we might have hope" (Rom. 15:4). Today we not only have that Old Testament witness but the entire New Testament too to encourage us. If people in past ages could hope, we have every reason to move ahead unafraid. Advent is a season that rekindles our hopes. We find new hope in God.

Lord, sometimes I grow discouraged and upset in life. You seem far away and my faith wavers. Teach me the importance of hope. Help me so that I never lose trust in you. Amen.

The Complete Picture

The Bible is a big book, in fact a library of sixty-six different books. The range of material in those sixty-six books is vast. You can find prose and poetry, shocking stories, wise philosophy, joyful promises, and terrible threats. Even within a single book like the book of Psalms, the variety of subjects is vast, covering almost every emotion and thought of human beings in some fashion.

This diversity is important for us to remember. It is easy to concentrate on one viewpoint and forget about the rest. Most of the false teachings that have upset the church have come about because men have done just this kind of one-sided study. Thus it is easy to speak about justice and to forget about love or to emphasize that man is a sinner and forget that by God's grace he can become a saint.

Psalm 42 can easily mislead if we aren't careful. The picture here is a sad one, a story filled with the cries of a man who has seen better days. One can easily deduce that the Christian life is one of sorrow and misunderstanding. But this psalm is just one phase of life; it is a part of the truth and not all of it. The Christian does face trouble and tribulation but there are also happy days and real blessings for those who love the Lord.

Most people are familiar with the story of the blind men and the elephant. They all tried to describe the elephant's appearance. One, taking hold of the tail, was sure the elephant was like a snake. Another, falling against the side of the beast, said the elephant was like a wall. A third, holding on to a leg, said the elephant was very much like a tree. At the end of the story we are told that all of the men were right and yet all of them were dead wrong.

That's what can happen if we overplay one aspect of truth. Jonathan Edwards who once frightened all of New England with his preaching was reminded by another clergyman that God was also a God of love, but Edwards didn't listen and thus misled many people with his terrible oratory. Balance and proportion is important in studying the Bible. We need the overall view.

Yet there are times when we need a particular stress, when one aspect can really touch our needs. To those in distress the 42nd psalm can be of great comfort, for it makes us realize that others have had troubles and have conquered them. And the concluding call, "Hope in God," can be and is good advice for all of us in Advent or at any time of the year.

Lord, help me to see the whole picture of truth as revealed in your word. Open my understanding so that I can grasp the deep sections of your word. Give me a love for the Bible so that I will study it and learn all that you have revealed. Amen.

O Praise Him

Praise! Praise the Lord. Praise the Lord? We have become so accustomed to the idea of praising God that the strangeness of it is lost on us. The 111th psalm is a praise psalm but that fact causes us no uneasiness. Why shouldn't we praise God?

And yet on second thought this seems a rather foolish activity. God is the creator and the ruler of all things. The entire universe is in his hands. He certainly doesn't need us to tell him how great he is. Indeed there is almost something scandalous about the idea of a God who likes to hear the tiny creatures on this earth sing about his power and might.

Dean Inge once said that he didn't know too much about God but he was sure God didn't like to be serenaded. Listening to some of our singing, we may be inclined to agree with the gloomy dean. What's our idea of praising God anyway? Why all the carols and songs of praise at Advent and Christmas?

Sometimes we can expose the falseness of a position by dealing with its opposite. Is it a *bad* thing to praise God? Would the psalmist have been a better man if he hadn't written this psalm? Are we more human if we are like the old New Englander who told his wife: "When I think of all you've meant to me over the years and all you've done for me, it's almost more than I can do to keep from telling you how much I love you."?

The answer is obvious. Praise is good for *us*. If we truly appreciate all the blessings we have received from God, it would be cruel and foolish to bottle it all up inside. We may not be able to say precisely the proper words, we may not be able to sing every syllable in tune, but it is good for us to praise God, even if our songs go no higher than the rooftops and even if God doesn't hear a word we say. In every season, but particularly in Advent we need to sing: "Praise to the Lord, the Almighty, the King of creation."

But let's not crowd God out of the picture. Of course he doesn't need our praise, any more than the wife in New England needed to be told that her husband loved her. But it would have been nice for her to hear. Husbands and wives appreciate kind words; parents like to be told that their children love and appreciate them. In a family, praise is not intended to build up pride or egotism; it's an expression of love.

And the same thing is true for our relationship to God. He is not a great and terrible ruler whom we seek to placate by compliments. He is a father, a member of our family. And so when we speak words of praise to him, we do so as children praising the one who has again and again shown his concern for us. The writer of Psalm 111 has the right stress for Advent and Christmas. Praise the Lord.

We praise you, God, and thank you for your love and concern for us. In this season we give you special thanks for the gift of your Son to us and for the promise of his return. Help us always to be ready for him and grateful to you. Amen.

116

The More We Get Together

Would you like to become a hermit? Sometimes when we get overwhelmed by the "rat race" of modern society, we feel like crawling in a hole and pulling the hole in after us. During the early history of Christianity some people did just that. Men and women retreated to lonely places in the desert and lived in isolation. The idea was that by living alone a person could concentrate on God and on holy things.

This move toward a hermit type of religion didn't succeed however, for Christianity is a community kind of faith. It requires contact with other human beings to be effective. After all, it doesn't do much good to talk about loving your brother if you never see him. The one who withdraws from the world also withdraws from God, who is in his world.

Perhaps the place where the community nature of our religion is most clearly shown is in *worship*. Notice that the psalmist declares that he is going to praise God "in the company of the upright in the congregation." He knew the importance of worshiping with others. No one needed to tell him to go to church or to join with others in praising God.

It's not hard to understand the importance of community worship. Christian people stimulate one another when they are together. One of the most appealing things about the Advent-Christmas season is the singing of familiar carols by a group of believers. Such singing has the same effect that you get when you build a fire with many logs instead of trying to use one that must burn by itself. Christian people need to get together.

But in addition, worshiping together is a witness to the world. It says, "We've got a good thing here. Come and join us." People who are not believers observe the rise and fall of church attendance just as much as Christians do. When asked how they became believers; a family in one of our large cities said, "We kept seeing our neighbors walk "past our house every Sunday at 7:15 P.M. Finally we asked them where they went each Sunday and they invited us to church. That's how we got started." You never know who may be influenced by your example in worship.

The psalmist then knew what all of us need to know—the more we get together, the closer we are to our fellow Christians and to God. Worship is not a duty, it's an opportunity. We don't need rules to make us go to church; we need an appreciation of the joy that comes in being with others. The Advent season reaches its height when we join with fellow believers at the manger in Bethlehem.

Lord, we thank you for the privilege of worshiping with others. Help us to share with all believers the good news of Christmas. Keep that spirit alive within us all the year ahead. Amen.

Do You See What I See?

Ebenezer Bryce, who discovered Bryce Canyon
and had it named after him, was once asked his reaction to that beautiful place. He replied, "As I remember, it was a bad place to lose a cow." We
shudder at such a reaction to the beauty of the canyon, but Bryce isn't alone in his blindness. The truth
is that people see what they want to see.

Notice what happens at Christmas. For some this
is a holy time, a joyous time, a time to celebrate the
birth of the Christ child. For others Christmas is a
drag, a season for work and bills and end-of-the-year
regrets. And for still others the holiday is for drunk-
enness and carousing. It all depends on what you see.

For if beauty is in the eye of the beholder, so is
meaning. Interpretation depends on the individual
more than on the event itself. So the psalmist speaks
about the greatness of the Lord's works, but he is
wise enough to recognize that this is the viewpoint
of those who have pleasure in God. The pleasure
must be there first or our reaction may be that of
boredom, not joy.

Jesus experienced this difference in interpretation
many times. When he performed miracles of healing,
some were impressed; others said he did all this
through Satan's power. Even when the news of the
resurrection was reported to his enemies, they were
not converted but busied themselves in working out
a plausible explanation for what had occurred.

119

This difference in viewpoint is important for Christians to understand. For when we note that some people don't get the same meaning from the Bible that we do, our faith is often shaken. If some scientist says that he doesn't believe in God, we begin to wonder if we are just ignorant dupes.

But it all depends on the starting place. If all that interests you is cows, you will react like Ebenezer Bryce and feel that a beautiful canyon is simply a terrible place to lose a cow. If you are not concerned with spiritual meanings, then Christmas is just the story of a peasant woman who had a child in an over-crowded town and so had to spend her time in a stable. It's only when your eyes are opened by the Holy Spirit that you can see the full meaning of God's truth.

Thus an unlearned individual may know more about spiritual things than the wisest non-believer. We always have to ask, as does a modern Christmas carol: "Do you see what I see? Do you hear what I hear?" And we shouldn't be too disturbed if the answer is: "No." For some see only a stable. Others see a king in a stable.

Lord, open my eyes to your truth. In this holy season help me to see in the coming of the Christ child the great witness of your love for me and for all mankind. Amen.

Preparing for a Memory

All the events of the Bible happened a long time ago, even those that are recorded in what we call the *New* Testament. While we can't exactly fix the year of Jesus' birth, we do know that more than 1900 years have passed since the angels sang to shepherds and wise men came to worship a new born king. Thus Advent in some ways seems like a foolish preparation. We are getting ready for something that has already happened. We are preparing for a memory.

But that's not right. Christian events are not just rooted in history in the same way as the Battle of Waterloo or the emancipation proclamation. The biblical events are a part of the today world for they keep repeating themselves in the life of each believer.

Phillips Brooks, the author of "O Little Town of Bethlehem," caught this truth in his famous carol. He wrote the text three years after he had visited the Holy Land and had spent some time in Bethlehem. But every line in the song is in the present tense. Note:

> The hopes and fears of all the years
> Are met in thee tonight.

And in the last verse:

> Cast out our sin, and enter in,
> Be born in us today.

It is as if time and space have ceased to exist and we are all participants in the Bible story.

The psalmist had this same feeling. In verses 4-6 of Psalm 111 the psalmist is referring to the fact that God delivered Israel from Egypt, fed her in the wilderness, and settled the people in the promised land. And yet the psalm speaks as if all this was happening at the moment the words were being written.

This timelessness is an essential part of our faith. Thus when we come to the communion table we are sure that Christ is there, waiting for us. When we celebrate the resurrection it is as if it has just happened and we are hearing the news for the first time.

So in Advent we too hear the call of John the Baptist, just as the people in the first century heard it. We feel the need to prepare the way for the coming of the King. And we too reflect the prayer Phillips Brooks uses at the close of his famous song:

> O come to us, abide with us,
> Our Lord Immanuel.

Lord, help us to feel your presence in our lives today. Don't let us push you into the past, don't let us think of you in terms of history but in terms of life. Be with us now, here, and in every moment of our life. Amen.

An Old, Established Firm

Founded, 1850. Founded, 1790. Founded, 1674. Business houses like to advertise the date they came into existence, particularly if the company has had a long history. For an early date shows that the firm has been a successful one. A long period of existence usually indicates that the company makes good products and gives reliable service. But above all, an early date makes us feel that the management has been trustworthy. No company can exist for any length of time if the people do not trust those in charge of the business.

For life is based on trust. When we hire a man to work for us, we must believe that he will work efficiently and honestly. When people marry, the marriage must be based on mutual trust or there is a speedy end to the arrangement. Even governments can't remain in power very long if people do not trust their leaders.

That's why the psalmist's words about trust are important. He is convinced that God is faithful and just and completely trustworthy in his dealings with people. And this opinion is confirmed by human history. The story of Israel certainly proves the psalmist's opinion. Again and again God made promises to his people and he always kept his word. The events of Christmas are just one example of God's trustworthiness.

Of course, we must not regard the Bible as a

kind of prophecy book, spelling out all future history. Nevertheless the prophecies which have been fulfilled do show God's reliability. God could certainly put up a sign advertising, "The Oldest Firm in Existence," and inscribe on it the motto, "You Can Trust Me."

This record of God's faithfulness is especially important in the Advent season. For during Advent we hear about an unfulfilled promise—the second coming. Jesus indicated plainly that there was another event on God's calendar, the return of Jesus as Lord and Judge.

Unfortunately we are tempted to doubt the truth of this promise. The centuries go on and nothing happens. Luther was sure in his day that the world could not continue for another hundred years and yet more than four hundred years have passed and still Christ has not returned. It all seems a bit hopeless.

But we need have no fear. The firm of God and Company has never gone back on a promise yet. The second coming has the same guarantees as the first one. The oldest firm in existence stands behind its promises. Our only concern is to make sure we are prepared when God gets ready to make good on his word.

Lord, teach me to trust completely in your word. Help me when I waver. Reassure me when I doubt. And if it be possible, come quickly to free this earth from the curse of sin. Amen.

The Beautiful Name

"God will forgive me. That's his trade." A witty Frenchman once said that and he didn't expect anyone to take him seriously. He knew as well as we do that you can't approach God with such an arrogant attitude. God will not be mocked.

And yet there is a sense in which the witty remark is true. God is a redeemer, a rescuer who extricates people from their troubles and forgives them for their follies. There isn't a more beautiful or accurate name for God than the word "Redeemer."

That's why the psalmist says that God sent redemption to his people. He recognized that the history of Israel is the history of redemption. The pattern is most clearly shown in that strange book, *Judges,* but it appears over and over again. Israel falls into sin, the people call on God for help, and God redeems the land. Certainly anyone reading the Old Testament would feel that redemption, forgiveness was God's trade.

The New Testament emphasizes the same truth. The name "Jesus" means savior or redeemer and that name was assigned to our Lord even before he was born, for Joseph was told, "He shall save his people from their sins." The whole significance and purpose of Advent is in this beautiful name *Redeemer.* If God is a God who redeems, then we need to get ready for the coming of our savior. If God doesn't redeem, we are wasting our time.

We are reminded of that old character Elijah in his contest with the priests of Baal. The false prophets called to their god all day but they got no results for Baal was not a redeemer, a god who could save. But Elijah only had to ask one time and the fire from heaven appeared. God can redeem.

Only we must remember that when the real work of redemption was begun, God did not send fire from heaven but came himself in the form of a baby in a manger. And although our thoughts now are concentrated on the Christmas story, we should not forget the cost of our redemption: "You were ransomed . . . not with perishable things such as silver and gold, but with the precious blood of Christ" (1 Peter 1:18-19). Even at Advent and Christmas we must not forget what it cost God to wear that beautiful name—Redeemer.

That's what Christmas is all about. As we hear again the familiar story of the coming of Christ, we are reminded of the name Redeemer. And the witty Frenchman was right. Only let's say it in more fitting language. God will redeem us. He does it because he is God.

Heavenly Father, we thank you for your redemption in Christ. We know we cannot repay you. We cannot really thank you as we should. But take us as we are, weak and faltering, and make us strong in Christ. Amen.

The Final Note

Psalm 111 seems to end on a sour note, at least on a note that isn't in harmony with our mood at Christmas time. The psalmist talks about the fear of the Lord and he speaks about God's name being holy and terrible. Even if you use a translation that softens the words slightly, the message seems a bit unpleasant and certainly not like the Christmas proclamation of a baby in swaddling clothes lying in a manger. After all, the angel's message was "fear not," rather than "fear God."

Yet perhaps this ending to the psalm is a fitting close to our Advent meditations. It reminds us that there is a difference between the world of the Old Testament and the New. God thundered at his people at Mt. Sinai and shut himself away from them in the Holy of Holies in the temple, where only the High Priest could come once a year. But in the New Testament he appears as a baby in a manger and as a man walking and talking to others.

This doesn't mean that there is no need for awe and respect in our day. At times we are tempted to picture God as an indulgent old grandpa, rather than as Lord and Savior. The description of God given by Omar Khayyam: "Pish! He's a Good Fellow, and 'twill all be well," finds no echo in either Testament. But Jesus did bring to us a new dimension of understanding about God. Jesus showed us God as

127

Father, Friend, Savior and we must never forget that picture.

But it is foolish to read too much into the word "fear." What the psalmist is saying is that God is a personal God and each of us must begin our religious life by acknowledging that fact. We must let God be God and we must accept him as *our* God. This personal note is struck at the very outset when the writer says "I will give thanks," and he ends his poem with an appeal to everyone to exhibit the same personal acceptance of God.

And this personal stress is particularly important as we move from Advent to the Christmas season. For carols and candles and even partridges in a pear tree will not cover up our spiritual poverty if God is not our personal God. The whole point of the Advent season is to make us look into our own heart deeply and see what God is to us. Jesus stressed this truth to his disciples when, after asking what others thought about him, he laid it on the line and asked, "Who do you say that I am?" He still asks that question of us today.

Someone once said that Christians must learn to read John 3:16 this way: "For God so loved me that he gave his only Son, so that if I believe in him, I shall not perish but have eternal life." Is that how you read it?

Come into my heart, come into my heart Lord Jesus. Come in today, come in to stay, come into my heart, Lord Jesus. Amen.